Silent **Revolution**

A daily Advent reflection

TONY CASTLE

Kevin
Mayhew

First published in 2001 by
KEVIN MAYHEW LTD
Buxhall, Stowmarket, Suffolk IP14 3BW
Email: info@kevinmayhewltd.com

All royalties from this book will be used in Bangladesh.

Scripture quotations taken from

Holy Bible, New International Version. Copyright © 1973,
1978, 1984 by International Bible Society. Used by permission
of Hodder & Stroughton Ltd.

Good News Bible, published by The Bible Societies/
HarperCollins Publishers Ltd, UK. © American Bible
Society, 1966, 1971, 1976, 1992.

9 8 7 6 5 4 3 2 1 0

ISBN 1 84003 785 7
Catalogue No 1500450

Cover design by Jonathan Stroulger
Edited by Sophia Sorrell
Typesetting by Richard Weaver

Printed and bound in Great Britain

Contents

*Dedicated to Cathy Clark
and my other fellow-travellers
Christopher Gallagher, Stephen King,
Stephen Atherton and Anne-Marie Coppock*

Foreword

Bangladesh is an Islamic country and Christian agencies that work there believe that it is important to respect the beliefs and the culture of the people. The Anglican Communion has a presence in the country. Its aid work is directed by the Christian Commission for Development in Bangladesh (CCDB), an organisation supported by Christian Aid. World Vision, the evangelical agency, is also very active in development work there. The Catholic Church represents the largest Christian presence in the country.

The Red Crescent (the Islamic version of the Red Cross) is engaged in relief work when it is necessary, and there are a number of large and well-financed Islamic aid or development agencies. Any agency, be it Islamic or Christian, which is not funded or controlled by the Government is called a 'non-government organisation' (NGO).

The Ahsania Mission, an Islamic NGO, is an excellent example of a large and professionally managed agency. It concentrates on educational provision, running teacher training colleges and adult education institutions. The Mission publishes a wide range of educational material to further adult education, especially among the poor and illiterate (approximately 60 per cent of the population can read and write).

In 2000 I visited Bangladesh with CAFOD (the Catholic Agency for Overseas Development) which is the official aid agency of the Roman Catholic Church of England and Wales (just as TEAR Fund is for the Non-conformist churches). It supports over 1,000 projects in 75 countries and works predominantly through local partners in these countries. Although it is the official agency of the Catholic Church, it does not just fund and support Catholic or Christian projects and initiatives but also those of other faiths.

Caritas* is CAFOD's main partner in Bangladesh; as the official agency of the Catholic Church of Bangladesh it is equivalent to CAFOD in England. It is through this Catholic agency that CAFOD funds most of its relief and development work in Bangladesh. However, it also supports the Ahsania Mission, the Islamic non-government organisation. Caritas Bangladesh is only one of many similar Catholic agencies around the world. Wherever the Catholic Church is established, the bishops have set up a Caritas agency. So there is a Caritas India, Caritas Australia, Caritas France, Caritas Holland, etc. The agencies in the wealthy northern hemisphere countries pass financial aid to those in the developing countries. While

* Caritas means 'love'.

we were staying in the guesthouse at Caritas, Dhaka, visitors came and went from several Asian Caritas agencies.

I was impressed to discover how well run CAFOD's partner agencies are, and by the professionalism of the staff I met from just some of the many Caritas agencies. Sadly, I also learnt that in spite of the hard work and dedication of many wonderful people, the need, as you will see from this diary, is still vast.

Introduction

How silently, how silently,
the wondrous gift is given!

When I was out with my family and some friends on Christmas Eve, carol singing in the local streets for the homeless, these two lines from 'O little town of Bethlehem' struck me. The most amazing, incredible event ever to happen in human history – words are hard to find to express the wonder of it – took place almost totally unnoticed! Impressive emperors and presidents, history-changing battles, life-enhancing inventions, saintly popes, etc., make a temporary stir; all come and go. But nothing comes near to what happened in a scruffy stable in a small insignificant Roman province 2,000 years ago. A poor, outwardly unremarkable couple took shelter one night and a boy child was born. Faith later informs us that this was no ordinary child, but the 'Word made Flesh'; God himself comes to be with us in human form. Now that's a staggering belief if you really stop and think about it!

How silently, secretly, God enters our world; and the great revolution begins. The world, the human race, is to be changed, turned upside down. That revolution is spelt out, according to Luke, in the very first public statement of Jesus of Nazareth in the local synagogue; quoting the words of the prophet Isaiah, he said –

> The Spirit of the Lord is on me,
>   because he has anointed me
>   to preach good news to the poor.
> He has sent me to proclaim freedom for the prisoners
>   and recovery of sight for the blind,
>   to release the oppressed,
>   to proclaim the year of the Lord's favour. (Luke 4:18-19)

The silent revolution, begun in a stable 30 or more years before, is now proclaimed. Three years later the religious and civil authorities – the powers of this world – try to silence it. They succeed in killing the messenger, but they fail to kill the message and stop the revolution . . .

In November 1999 I saw an advertisement placed by CAFOD (Catholic Agency for Overseas Development) inviting teachers in England and

Wales to apply for a place on a Millennium project. CAFOD had received a grant from the Millennium Commission to send ordinary people – community activists, youth leaders and teachers – to a poor developing country to experience life there. (In the first year of the scheme 16 community activists travelled abroad for three weeks; in 1998 the same number of youth leaders went.) In 1999 CAFOD were looking for 16 teachers to sample life in Kenya, Zambia, Peru and Bangladesh to witness the relief and development projects in those countries.

After some doubts I applied. In December I learnt that 450 teachers had sought places and was pleased to be informed that I was shortlisted. Forty-five of us attended the CAFOD central office in South London in February for an interview and in March I was elated to be informed that I was one of the 16 'awardees'. A few weeks later, at our first training weekend, I was told that I was going to Bangladesh. At first I was a little disappointed, because I fancied the idea of Peru. However, an experienced friend who had already been to Bangladesh assured me that visiting an Islamic society would be more interesting; as it proved to be.

After very thorough and sound training and preparation, we, four teachers, with two CAFOD staff in a leadership role, set out on the 12-hour flight to Bangladesh. It was to be an enriching and life-changing experience.

We needed to produce a full report of all our activities and experiences for the Millennium Commission, so, at the end of each day we tried to give time to recording that day's events. Then, just before going to bed, I spent about 45 minutes writing up my own personal diary. That diary forms the substance of this Advent book.

From the very beginning of our visit, and several times in the course of it, people spoke of 'a silent revolution' that is gradually taking place in Bangladesh. It arises primarily from the advancement of women, in and through the many hundreds of women's groups that meet regularly throughout the country.

One of the most humbling of experiences – and there were many such – was to sit on the ground in a group circle, talking with these struggling, but determined women. We listened with respect and admiration to their account of their efforts to fight poverty, an inadequate, often poisoned water supply, limited sanitation provision, lack of steady employment, unjust pay for long hours of work, fear of leaving their homes after dark and so on. And all the while they maintained a wonderful dignity and quiet self-confidence, peppered with a good sense of humour.

I sensed, and was not alone in this, a great air of expectation, particularly in the groups and in the countryside, where most of the people live.

It was silently there in the women's groups, among the young people and among the educated field workers that we talked with. Bangladesh is, in my opinion, an Advent country. A young country – only coming into being in 1971 – which waits in expectation. It will be from the women – as from Mary herself – that salvation will come.

> *No ear can hear his coming:*
> *but in this world of sin,*
> *where meek souls will receive him, still*
> *the dear Christ enters in.*

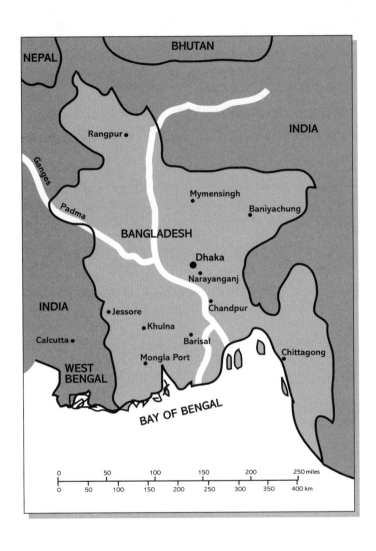

NEPAL

BHUTAN

INDIA

Rangpur •

Ganges

Padma

Mymensingh
•

Baniyachung
•

BANGLADESH

Dhaka •
Narayanganj •

INDIA

• Jessore

Chandpur •

• Khulna

Calcutta •

Barisal •

Chittagong •

WEST
BENGAL

Mongla Port •

BAY OF BENGAL

0	50	100	150	200	250 miles
0	50	100	150	200	250	300	350	400 km

Bangladesh

On the map opposite you will notice that, apart from the Bay of Bengal and an area to the south-east, Bangladesh is totally surrounded by India. The former province of Bengal was divided into West and East Bengal in 1947; the latter becoming Bangladesh after a dreadful war of independence in 1971.

It is approximately the same size as England and Wales, but has well over twice the population. Of the population of 120 million, 35 per cent live below the poverty line (so approximately the equivalent of the population of England lives in poverty).

You will also notice, looking at the map, that the River Ganges becomes the Padma river once it enters Bangladesh. It is a very wide river and only one of the many rivers, waterways, lakes, ponds and streams that are to be found in the alluvial plain, which constitutes most of the country. Much of the countryside routinely floods during the summer monsoon season, so you see everywhere little villages and settlements on raised 'islands', and the roadways are all raised up. The people are accustomed to the annual flooding – in fact the fertility of the land, which yields three rice harvests a year, depends on it.

Not shown on the map, but up in the right-hand corner, east of Mymensingh, is Sylhet, where there are tea plantations. This area has the nickname 'Little London' in Bangladesh, because it is Bengali people from this area who immigrate to Britain.

Up at Rangpur and north of Mymensingh, the countryside becomes hilly with far fewer waterways and ponds. Members of our group (not the author) visited Chittagong and the hill country to the south-east. Here the tribal people, who are not Bengali, live and are in constant conflict over land rights. In the north, close to Mymensingh, is the Modhupur forest which is one of the last sizeable rain forests in Asia; here too the tribal people live.

A larger forest, the Sundarban, is south of Khulna; there is much protected wildlife and 'Uncle' – the local nickname for the Royal Bengal tiger – roams free.

The constitution of the country guarantees religious freedom to all. The people are very religious in outlook, 83 per cent being Muslim, 10 per cent Hindu, and there are small Christian and Buddhist communities.

Politically the People's Republic of Bangladesh is a democratic country with, currently, a woman prime minister. The role and place of women in society is slowly improving; they have recently been admitted to the armed forces. The language of the country, over which the war of independence was fought in 1971, is Bengali or Bangla, although a small number speak tribal dialects. English is taught in most schools and most educated people can converse in English. The historical link with Britain is still seen on the roads where driving is on the left – officially!

Bangladesh is one of the world's poorest and most densely populated countries. Many people are landless and are forced to live on and cultivate the flood-prone land. There is very limited access to a safe water supply. The economy is largely agricultural with the cultivation of rice being the single most important activity. There are some tea plantations in the north-eastern region.

The best and most popular time of the year to visit Bangladesh is late October to early November, when the climate is very agreeable and the rice crop is being gathered. It is a very beautiful, unspoilt country, with gentle and very hospitable people.

DAY ONE

Send-off

It had seemed distant and unreal; going to far-away Bangladesh for three weeks, all expenses paid by the Millennium Commission. The training by CAFOD, which I had taken seriously, had been good and thorough, but somehow the trip had still seemed unreal. The three teachers whom I had first met at the training weekends and who were to be my travelling companions, seemed very pleasant and easy to get on with. Now, suddenly, it was all very real! It first hit me when I started laying out on the bed all the items on my list: the clothes and the equipment. Instead of being energised by this, as I thought I would be, I was strangely reluctant and almost inert.

Perhaps reality now meant parting with the safe, the secure and the comfortable. It would be the first time in 27 years of marriage that Liz and I would be apart for more than a week. I felt sure all the household jobs I usually looked after – cleaning the kitchen floor, emptying the bins, unstacking the dishwasher and so on – would be well looked after. What strange things we think of at a time like this.

The family waved me off at 5.30pm from my sister-in-law's wedding reception at the Woodman in Blackfen, south-east London. The traffic was very heavy and the taxi took two hours to find the Ibis hotel on the Bath Road close to Heathrow airport. This was where we were going to meet up and spend the night. I was not the last to arrive. The two Stephens were delayed but arrived in time for dinner. For some reason or other I felt rather 'remote' from my companions, although I tried to socialise and be chatty. After a pleasant dinner and a few drinks together we retired to our rooms at 11pm. Although I felt a little nervous about things I slept well. The others reported that they had a disturbed night.

Reflection

It was pouring with rain and I had a sinking feeling as I waited for the taxi. For a few moments I didn't want to go; the warmth and security of the music and laughter behind me at the wedding reception were so much more inviting. That was where my family was and I was going with virtual strangers to a far away, desperately poor country; what was the point of it?

Then suddenly the taxi was there and my wife and children were hugging me and wishing me a safe journey. They did not know how choked I felt as I waved goodbye.

Advent reflection

Leaving behind the familiar and embracing the new and the challenging is what Advent is about. We try to make and keep our lives comfortable, believing, mistakenly, that comfort means happiness: our common pursuit. But old shoes that are comfortable, moulded to our feet, often let in the rain. Habits that ensure a smooth and comfortable life can fall short of what Christ, Our Lord, asks of us.

Scripture text

'Comfort my people,' says our God. 'Comfort them!'
. . . A voice cries out, 'Prepare in the wilderness a road for the Lord.
Clear the way in the desert for our God.'
Isaiah 40:1-3

Prayer

Father, Eternal Wisdom,
    it was according to your plan and design
    that silently and barely noticed
    your Son would enter our world.
His coming changed everything.
As we consider his advent
    may we be prepared to be challenged?
May we heed the call of the Baptist,
    to clear the way and be prepared
    to think new thoughts and consider
    new ways of relating to you and one another. Amen

DAY TWO

Departure

A minibus taxi collected us from the hotel at 7.30am, and with little delay we found ourselves in the departure lounge of Terminal 4 at Heathrow. There were a lot of Indian people in the line for our flight; in fact, apart from a young couple with rucksacks, I could see no other European passengers. Our leader, Stephen, collected our passports and got us through quickly as a group. Steve was excited and nervous because this was only his second time on an aircraft. (We had agreed that with two 'Stephens' on our trip, Stephen King, our leader, would have the full title and Stephen Atherton would be 'Steve'.)

The 12-hour flight did not seem as long as I had expected; but then I did watch three films on the personal small screen in front of me! We had discovered that there was to be an hour's stop at Calcutta. Eager to say that we had been to India, and having an opportunity to stretch our legs, we all took the option of getting off. It was a mistake – or a memorable experience – whichever way you want to view it. First we sat in a grubby bus for 15 minutes while we waited for something to happen and, when delivered to the reserved area, we walked up into a deserted and desolate hall with rows of plastic chairs. At least, I thought, here's a chance to walk around and get a little exercise. Having a small bottle of water, I also took the opportunity to clean my teeth.

We waited around for about 30 minutes and then the Indian security people insisted on a security check – eight of them to only about 14 passengers. Their X-ray machine was not working; so it became a manual check, looking through our hand luggage. I put the small blue box of homeopathic medicines, lent to me by Mr Collin our local chemist, in clear view on a table while I was given a body search. I moved it across to the bench where our bags were being searched, all in full view. No one asked what the box was or what it contained, although it was big enough to contain a gun or explosives. After my hand luggage had been checked I picked the blue box up and put it back in my small rucksack. So much for Indian security. As I was returning to the plane I was sent back from the exit because the security man responsible had not stamped my boarding card, presumably recording that I had been processed.

We landed 30 minutes later at Dhaka and quickly cleared immigration. There were large puddles outside the terminal (they had had a small cyclone) and police, armed with rifles, stood about. Two cars, with four men from Caritas, arrived to welcome us. It was an experience to see in the semi-darkness the gaudy rickshaws plying their trade at 4.30 in the morning, as we drove through the city. We arrived at the Caritas compound at about 5am, to a great welcome. I was given a room on the first floor and one of my first tasks was to sort out the mosquito net around the bed.

Reflection

When is security secure? When it's observant, I would suggest. The best police officer, customs officer or security guard is the one who sees all and can interpret correctly what she or he sees.

Advent reflection

Human beings need to feel secure; that's how the insurance companies flourish. Some people are frightened of the dark; because they cannot see they feel insecure. On an aircraft we cannot usually see the pilot, but we trust that he is there and that he knows what he is doing. It is the same in our spiritual lives: there is much that we cannot see and understand, but our trust is in God, who sees all. Advent provides us with the opportunity to take a serious look at our trust; do I place all my trust in the God who loves us so much that he gave us his own dear Son?

Scripture text

Keep me safe, O God, for in you I take refuge.
Lord, you have assigned me my portion and my cup;
    you have made my lot secure.
Psalm 16:1, 5

Prayer

Father, we know that you desire
    our happiness and our security.
Many frightening things happen in our lives,
    over which we have no control,
    and often we feel that we are left in the dark.
Father, be our security.
Help us to place all our trust in you. Amen

DAY THREE

Dhaka traffic

It's 10am and I've just surrendered to the constant loud honking of horns, to discover that the whole world of rickshaws pass my window at the back of the room (double-glazed). I'm having a banana for breakfast, as I write. It's very warm but overcast and large puddles can be seen outside in the courtyard where the vehicles are parked.

My room has a concrete floor and a grubby Indian carpet in the centre; a large ceiling fan and a shower room off. It has a toilet, handbasin and shower; the shower is in the centre of the room and the water runs away to one corner and disappears. (Now I know why we were advised to bring flip-flops.) The never-ending river of humanity perched on rickshaws flows past with the loud ringing of bicycle bells. Early this morning I got entangled in the mosquito net, but I haven't seen a mosquito yet . . .

The rest of the morning was spent going over the proposed programme with Benedict and Albert, two of the Caritas Bengali directors. The seriousness, commitment and enthusiasm of the Caritas executives are very apparent. Lunch in the canteen, rice, fish and vegetables.

After a meeting of our group to sort out how we are going to record each day and write up our final report, we were taken out by Aziz, the centre's driver, into the traffic of the city. What an incredible experience! It was 5pm and rush hour, and what a rush! There were tens of thousands of colourful rickshaws (with a lean male cyclist wearing a sarong and flip-flop sandals powering each) all over the place, coming at us from all angles, their bells ringing. Mixed up with them were baby taxis. These are highly decorated larger vehicles that carry as many as you can jam in and are driven by a two-stroke scooter engine which belches out petrol fumes. Mix in the occasional, crowded-with-humanity battered bus, the brightly decorated heavy lorry and the very occasional car and there you have it; rush hour in Dhaka and a hell of a jam.

The sights were so many and so various; often the rickshaws had three or even four people jammed in the two seats, or huge bales of straw, or pieces of furniture or whatever. There were pedestrians ducking and weaving their way through the jostling-for-space vehicles, everyone honking their horns or ringing their bicycle bells. It was a nightmare scene, a fight for survival; yet, and this was surprising and we all commented on it, there was no bad temper and everyone appeared to patiently accept the chaos. There seemed to be very few rules of the road, and it was obvious that no one took any notice of red traffic lights and no one was prepared to give way – brute force won every time. I sat in the front alongside Aziz the driver, and wondered at his amazing driving skills. The experience lasted an hour.

During that short trip we saw so many other sights. A young mother's naked child, perhaps about a year or 18 months old, was sitting on the curb while she, ignoring the noisy traffic, washed clothes in a large puddle in the gutter. Two women on their haunches were shifting through a pile of filthy rubbish alongside the only European-type shop in the street, Sony, with TVs for sale. Poor families prepared for a night on the pavement by park railings, while posters above their heads praised the use of the Internet.

After dinner most of us went out again in the minibus to visit the Sheraton hotel. Steve had brought some gifts from home for a friend who was working in a Dhaka hospital, and they had arranged to meet in reception. I wasn't keen to go to a 'posh' hotel because it seemed an abuse of what we were there for – visiting relief and development work for the poor. However, I didn't want to be left behind and appear a killjoy. We had one drink, bought some postcards and returned.

Reflection

There appeared to be such utter chaos on the roads because simple rules of the road were not being observed. Why continue to have traffic lights if they are meaningless because no one obeys them? Any society or community that does not respect rules and laws is going to descend into chaos.

Advent reflection

It was because Adam and Eve, our first parents, did not respect the rules set by God in the Garden that chaos followed. Christ, the second Adam, whose coming we are preparing to celebrate, gave obedience to his Father; his faithfulness resulted in order being restored. Our lives often appear chaotic because we don't keep the first and most basic rule which is to ask, 'What is it that God wants me to do?' What fits most surely with the commandments? 'Love the Lord your God and your neighbour as yourself'?

Scripture text

People of Jerusalem . . . build a road for your returning people!
Put up a signal so that the nations can know . . .
That the Lord is coming to save you!
Isaiah 62: 10-11

Prayer

Father, Creator, it is not red lights
    to stop us, that we need.
We need the green for 'go';
    to go on, every day,
    seeking your will;
    and we need the energy
    and strength to do that will,
    today and every day. Amen

DAY FOUR

Beggars' hands to workers' hands

Woke up; put on the ceiling fan and took out my earplugs to be immediately bombarded with street bells and horns – another day in Dhaka! Cold shower after a hard bed – should toughen me up! After breakfast, out through the thronged streets again to the National Museum. It sounded like a pretty boring expedition but it proved to be important for an understanding of Bangladesh – and more interesting than any of us had expected.

Originally a magnificent building set in its own grounds, it is now run-down and in obvious need of funds. All the exhibits are poorly displayed (by our standards). After birds – the national bird is the magpie-robin – and plants, including jute and the national fruit, the jackfruit, we looked at musical instruments we'd never seen before and inspected displays of Bangla literature and poetry.

Then we came to the rooms dedicated to the war of Independence, 1971. The war, fought over the Bangla language, claimed 3 million lives before the Pakistan army surrendered on 16 December 1971. The photos on show and the news reports of the time were very graphic and harrowing, especially the sculpture of a dead body, half-encased in mud, called 'In Memory of '71 – Massacre of the Intellectuals'. One or two of the photos, especially of people living in drainage pipes, I remembered seeing in our national press 29 years ago.

Other less disturbing facts: there were, once upon a time, 7,000 different types of rice in the world and 4,000 of them were in Bangladesh. Only 40 now survive in the country.

In the north of the country at Paharpar the archaeological remains of the largest Buddhist monastery on the Indian subcontinent have been discovered. It had cells for 177 monks and dates from the eighth to the eleventh century, considered the Golden Age of Bangladesh.

As the only group of white visitors to the museum we were followed and stared at by an assortment of interested young people as though we were one of the exhibits. They sometimes looked for an opportunity to speak. A young boy of about 10 'adopted' me and trailed around behind me for half an hour. I regretted not having any sweets (left in the car) to give him when we left.

Next on, through the crazy traffic to Corr, the jute works. Down a muddy, wet and bumpy side road, past very impoverished workplaces to the works. A warm welcome from the director, Subash Rosario and his deputy, Mrs Bertha Gity Baroi. After a very tasty lunch in the boardroom we were shown round the works. In different rooms and 'halls' various activities, from quality control to candle-making, were going on. I took photos and spoke to a group of five giggling 16-18 year old girls. We were taken into the showroom and then the warehouse where we spent quite a lot of time selecting artefacts and gifts.

Back in the director's room we were shown the export awards the company has won in recent years from the government. (It supplies companies like Habitat and Ikea.) Caritas set up the jute works to employ poor women and war widows after the 1971 war; it is now independent and self-financing with 6,000 women outworkers. An impressive place that appeared to be well run.

Through the unbelievable rush hour traffic; it was 5pm by now. Stuck in a traffic jam we were accosted by a young mother with her baby who pleaded and begged and tapped on the window. I felt terrible sitting there holding my camera, only a foot from her face. Christ's words, 'What you do for the least person, you do for me', came to mind, but we had been told not to give to beggars.

Stephen gave her a handful of sweets but that didn't satisfy her and we were only saved by the traffic eventually moving on. The experience led to a group discussion later that evening, and an agreement that we needed to give people a hand up, not a hand out. After more discussion, we worked out that the jute workers were earning £3 a week. We spent the remainder of the evening dividing the gifts we had brought with us into four carrier bags; we'll decide, as we go, whom to give them to.

Reflection

The most abiding memory is not likely to be of the National Museum or the jute works, but of the young mother begging by tapping on the car window. Hard as it is, it must be more correct to help people help themselves by giving them a hand up, rather than a hand-out. But are we really doing the former? Or is it a cop out?

Advent reflection

Are we seeking happiness for ourselves this Christmas, or for others? In our society we have none who need to beg because the state is supposed to make provision. But does that mean that there are *no* people in need of a 'hand up'? people who have suffered social, physical or mental hardship and need encouragement and support? Surely there are many such: the immigrants and asylum seekers. (Were not Mary, Joseph and Jesus asylum seekers in Egypt? Scripture is silent about who gave them a 'hand up'.) There are the 'rough-sleepers' on our streets and the women and children who have suffered domestic violence and are taking refuge in hostels, etc.

How can we give some of these a 'hand up' this Christmas?

Scripture text

And Mary said 'My soul glorifies the Lord
and my spirit rejoices in God my Saviour,
for he has been mindful of the humble state of his servant.'
Luke 1:46-48

Prayer

It seems utterly amazing, Lord,
that you, the creator of the vast universe,
came to this tiny insignificant planet,
to be one of us!
It is equally astonishing that when you came
you came to share not just our humanity,
but also the inequalities and indignities of the poor.
Your mother was not married when she conceived.
There was only a rough stable available for the birth.
The poorest of the Jewish people, the shepherds,
were the first visitors.
The authorities sought the death of the child,
and the family became asylum seekers in Egypt.
Lord; open our eyes and our hearts to the message
that you are trying to convey to us. Amen

DAY FIVE

The silent revolution

Struggled again, as I got up, with the all-embracing mosquito net. Ear plugs out: traffic bells and deafening horns; another new day in Dhaka. (I have developed a rough, dry cough which could be caused by the pollution of the city.) After our own briefing meeting, we met for a three-hour session with all the directors of Caritas – an impressive body of men (we noted that there were no women present). After introductions from both sides there was a presentation by each of the men – on the history of Bangladesh, the politics, the position of the Catholic Church in the country, the disaster relief programme, the education development programme, etc. It was my turn to be the scribe and I was kept very busy!

There was such a lot of information flowing from the worthy gentlemen that it became almost indigestible. The only piece that really registered – and I think I will always remember – was under the heading, *Signs of Hope*. Doctor Thomas Costa spoke of the 'silent revolution' that was producing a powerful social movement; women were becoming more and more empowered. The hundreds of women's groups around the country were heightening awareness and giving confidence to women; Caritas, supported by CAFOD, had been involved in the pioneering of these women's groups.

The meeting concluded with a good question-and-answer session. Over lunch I chatted with the new assistant press officer, Amol, whose wife was expecting a baby.

After lunch and a change of clothes, Stephen King, Cathy and I went off to visit the local bishop, Theotonius Gomes, and Sister Eugenia, at the office of the Bishops' Conference of Bangladesh. The others headed for the Notre Dame College and the Inter-Faith Library recently established there. The bishop was wonderfully open and relaxed, and Sister Eugenia gave the impression of being a very dedicated lady. Both were very interested in the award scheme that had brought us to Bangladesh, and the work of CAFOD, which they praised. We discussed the role of the Catholic Church in an Islamic culture and relations with those of that Faith. (There are seven bishops, 200 priests and 700 religious sisters.)

I asked Sister Eugenia about ecumenical relations with other Christian communities. She told us that these were very good and that an ecumenical event to mark the Millennium was planned for January. She said that they worked quite closely with the small Anglican Church which was led by

Bishop Dizen Barnabas Mandal. They had 27 parishes and some schools and hostels.

Interestingly, Sister Eugenia also spoke of a 'silent revolution' which is taking place for the empowerment of women. It was clear that she had worked tirelessly on inter-faith dialogue and she was keen for me to keep in touch. I promised a copy of my book *Christian Wisdom*, for the new inter-faith library.

After a group photo in the grounds we left for a visit to the archbishop. As we had arrived early at his compound, we strolled around the beautiful grounds admiring the vegetables and plants and visiting the seminary at the bottom of his garden. We met and spoke with the rector and one of his staff. Our colleagues who had visited the Notre Dame High School for Boys now arrived to inform us that we had a dinner date that evening with the priests of Notre Dame College. On the terrace of Archbishop's house, with a beautiful sunset behind us, we chatted with the informally dressed Archbishop Michael Rozario, a tall and energetic 72-year-old. He was relaxed and easy to speak to, and open to any topic, including the question of married priests; he appeared quite well-informed about the former Anglican married priests serving in English parishes. He told the old joke of how at the next Vatican Council the bishops will take their wives; at the Council after that the Pope will take her husband! After more tea and Madeira cake we left, bestowing CAFOD posters and booklets on the Archbishop as we withdrew.

On the way to the meal at Notre Dame College, in the gloom, I could see people – families I guessed – settling down for the night on the pavements, under plastic sheeting or large old woven mats, for some privacy from the throng of road-users. We were accosted yet again by the same beggars in the traffic snarl-up at the same junction. At Notre Dame we had a look at the inter-faith library which was being used, at the time, by about eight students. We then visited the Slum School: three sessions after normal school hours, with 400 attending each of the sessions and staffed by students of Notre Dame who, unable to pay any fees, did this work in the evenings instead. We walked into the sparse, large classrooms and spoke to the children who got very excited by our visit. I tried, not very successfully, to speak to 9-year-old Shahidha from the slums, and looked at her exercise book where she had skilfully drawn a hen and a dog. I wrote my name in pencil, alongside hers in her book and took her photo. This is the only schooling she can get because she has to work by helping her mother during the day. I also met her friends, Perivim and Shenmin. It was the most moving experience up to that point. The children came out of class and we were mobbed!

Upstairs in the College, we went into the priests' sitting-room and met four American Holy Cross priests (also a visiting Jesuit from Rome, Fr Tom Michel, the Pope's advisor on Islam). The four Americans were very interesting men, who had each dedicated over 40 years to Bangladesh and for many years they had considered it 'home'. One, Father James Banas, said, 'This is my country'. He retired from teaching and now runs the Notre Dame Rehabilitation Centre for Drug addicts; I spent most of my time talking to him. We had a drink with the priests and a simple meal. It was late when we returned to Caritas and we still had our reports to write. By the time I had written this account, it was 12.10am and time to grapple with the mosquito net.

Reflection

After so many tales in the press of Catholic priests who have failed the trust of their people, it was very inspiring and uplifting to spend time with such mature, dedicated priests. The experience gave even more point to 'the signs of hope' that we had heard about earlier in the day.

We must wait and see as we visit the women's groups; is there really a 'silent revolution' taking place among the women of Bangladesh, are there 'signs of hope'?

Advent reflection

Mother Teresa of Calcutta once said, 'God does not ask us to be successful, only faithful'. It is wonderfully encouraging to meet fellow Christians who have given faithful service over many years. Advent is when we recall the faithful ones of Judaism who had looked and longed for the appearing of the Messiah. As the Greek world and the Roman world celebrated their great historical events, the 'faithful' of Israel silently, patiently waited for the Messiah, Emmanuel, 'God-with-us'. That appearing would be a world-changing event, a true but silent revolution.

Scripture text

For my eyes have seen your salvation,
    which you have prepared in the sight of all people,
    a light for revelation to the Gentiles
    and for glory to your people Israel!
(*Words of the prophetic Simeon*) Luke 2:30-32

Prayer

Dear God of the ages,
    you take time over your work,
    and never appear to be in a hurry.
You are true to your promises.
We, time-bound creatures, are constantly
    in a hurry, looking for instant results and success.
Help us to appreciate the importance of faithfulness,
    of patience and perseverance.
May we, this Advent, take our time
    over our prayers and over the time we give to others,
    as we await the day when we celebrate
    your appearance among us. Amen

DAY SIX

Inter-faith concern for the poor

Up, reluctantly, at 7am for a departure at 8am to MAWTS (Mirpur Agricultural Workshop and Training School), the engineering school for 150 boys from poor families. After a drive to the outskirts of Dhaka we met with the director, Mr Innocent D'Costa, and his department managers. We learnt about the history of the establishment – an old factory purchased by Caritas in 1972 and up and running as a training school by 1976. Each year about 1,200 boys, all school dropouts from around the country apply, and 50 are selected. They train for three years and live in a hostel on site. All the managers of the school had been boys there. I met and took a photo of Al-haz Nazral Islam, a foreman, who showed me a hand-held syringe and needle crusher which they had designed, and make for local hospitals.

My camera's battery packed up during the day, so I used Cathy's while she took notes. Lads were working on lathes, old cars, and a wide range of other activities. The colour of the name labels on their blue overalls denotes their year; yellow for first year, then green and then red. The training school is self-financing through the products they make and sell. For example, we saw a potato selector and a small mobile water tank. Mr Haroun, a Muslim, who is in charge of the boys' welfare, impressed me. He showed us the dormitories; one for each year. He and his family live on site. On the wall of the staff room was a poster with these words, which we all commented on: *Judge each day, not by the harvest, but by the seeds you plant.*

We left the training school and walked to one side of it to where Caritas are building a new silk production plant and showrooms. We all took photos of the stonebreakers, under umbrellas, and male and female hod carriers. In the silk display room Steve, Chris and I selected saris to take home.

We were late arriving for lunch at the Caritas regional office (which has a most attractive inner courtyard lush with greenery). Another great welcome was given to us and the key workers sat down with us to lunch. Another tasty meal: some rice, but also chips and potatoes boiled in their skins; little crispy pieces of fish and small bony pieces of chicken and, this was the surprise, lovely big prawns in a 'hot' sauce. It was a great shame that we couldn't stop longer to continue our conversations, but we were due at the Ahsania Mission. (An Islamic NGO that receives funds from CAFOD, especially for an adult literacy programme.)

We all felt that at first our welcome at Ahsania was rather cool, but this may have been more from a sense of wariness, on their part, because we were Christian and they were Muslim. But, whatever the cause, as the two-hour visit progressed, it became very cordial. We met the key project directors and watched a video of their very extensive work – they are the largest supplier of adult education in the country. Steve, who was filming with his camcorder asked for a copy of the video and Chris, who had admired their posters on show round the room, asked if we could have copies to take home. (A roll was given to us as we left.) By this time we were all enjoying a joke together.

I asked about the trafficking of women and children, having seen some posters about it, and they confirmed that approximately 100 a month disappeared. Here too the phrase 'silent revolution' was used in connection with the gradual education of the women.

Downstairs we visited their well-resourced reference library which had an extensive collection of their publications to advance adult literacy. As we were shown round people smiled and said 'good afternoon'. The Ahsania directors really wanted us to give them two days, in order to take us round some of their many projects, and they were very disappointed when we told them that our programme was already full.

They did, however, take us to a Teachers' Training College that they run. It was down a narrow city street and hardly recognisable as an educational establishment. (We were told that this was the best in Dhaka. It led to a comment from Cathy: 'Is it not interesting that it takes three years to train a lad in an engineering works and one year to train a teacher!') We met staff and sat round a large table in their staff room, enjoying mysty (a sugary concoction) and tea (here, as has often been the case, you had to work hard to follow what was being said). Finally we went along a narrow corridor to a large classroom where graduates and postgraduates (some of them already teaching) were having a lecture on maths. I arrived last, because I had been showing my family-photos to three of the teachers. Just inside the door were two beautiful young teachers in saris. (Graduates with a BA degree each, they were now working for their BEd diplomas.) I got talking to them while the others were talking to other small groups and I showed my family-photos again; afterwards they asked me to write my name and address on their notepads and I took their names (one was called 'Lovely'; the other Mala). Both are Catholics and teach at the Maria Bambina Convent, Dhaka.

We got back 'home', to Caritas, in time to unwind a little before dinner. We wrote up our reports until 9pm when we tried to phone home, but without success.

Reflection

The dedication of the Christian directors at MAWTS and the equal dedication of the Muslim directors of Ahsania Mission conveyed important messages. Clearly the faith of both groups dictate their very obvious commitment to the plight of the poor. Faith in and love for the same God could, should, form the basis of more mutual trust, co-operation and respect.

Advent reflection

The Father sent his Son for all, not just for Christians. We Christians are so often guilty of being possessive of Christ. It is true that Muslims, for example, only accept Jesus of Nazareth as a great prophet, but he does not cease to be there for them.

Scripture text

See, darkness covers the earth and thick darkness is over the peoples,
    but the Lord rises upon you and his glory appears over you.
Nations will come to your light
    and kings to the brightness of your dawn!
Isaiah 60:2-3

Prayer

Lord of all nations and all peoples,
    your loving care is for all,
    regardless of race, religion or social condition.
You love Muslims, Jews and Hindu people,
    along with Christians of all the different traditions;
    you have no favourites.
May we imitate your love
    and show equal respect to all,
    for we are all your children. Amen

Mosque and market

Slept fitfully, and poor Chris told us at breakfast that he hadn't slept at all! After breakfast and a bit of packing, Stephen, Cathy and I waved goodbye to the others and set out for Khulna. A mile down the road, in all the noisy traffic, I found that my camera was missing and Aziz turned the car round. I soon found the camera and we were off again. Our flight to Jessore – rather a rough-and-ready check-in procedure – was only 25 minutes, but we still got a cookie and an orange drink!

The one-and-a-half-hour drive that followed (in a Toyota Spacecruiser) was fascinating and very interesting – there was so much to see and so much to photograph (but I tried to be selective, not having brought enough films with me). Everywhere, wherever there was a clear and flat piece of land, we saw the local boys playing cricket. A warm welcome awaited us at the Caritas Khulna office and we had a good lunch of rice with pieces of fish and, of course, bananas. After a short siesta, we travelled to see the ancient fifteenth-century mosque of 60 pillars and 87 domes, all in red brick (of which there is plenty around here). We took our shoes off and went into the cool of the white-painted mosque although there was not much to see. Cathy was angrily asked to leave by the tall bearded custodian; after intercession, he relented and allowed her to stand just inside the door!

Looking around the outside, I got talking to a group of about 14 stone-cutters, through Francis, the Caritas regional director. At first I thought that they were just cutting bricks up – as we had seen by the roadside before – but these were skilled men from the national archaeological team restoring the fabric of the mosque. They travel from site to site; and expected to be on their present job for another month.

The visit, 10 minutes later, to the local country market was mind-blowing. Words like fascinating, interesting, etc., don't convey the cultural experience it was. All local produce was being displayed – laid out on the ground, weighed with hand-held scales and haggled over. We caused quite a stir – many had not seen white people before and just stared. Quite a number wanted to say 'hello' but some of the young children were frightened of us!

We took a few photos but there was so much that one could have taken. I spoke in English to a young local farmer, whose name I didn't get. He spoke about what he grew, etc., and was clearly pleased to use his English.

A beggar, who was dumb, kept coming up and touching my hands and my feet; it was hard to shake him off (Francis spoke firmly to him, but I was confused – sorry for him, but anxious about his behaviour). There was a handicapped man there too, in a wheelchair, Shamin, whom Francis knew and introduced us to. He is a co-ordinator in Khulna for services to the disabled.

At the end of the market area was the Khan Jahan Ali Mazar mosque and shrine – a holy place – right beside a very large pond, or lake. Khan Jahan had been a famous holy man and leader in the fifteenth century and his followers had dug out the lake. Legend has it that there are two crocodiles in it – but we didn't see any sign of them. People were going in and out of the shrine, some giving food to a line of beggars by the wall.

We returned promptly to Khulna because we had a 5pm appointment with Bishop Michael D'Rozario (75 years of age). He was charming and after drinks and mysty (that candyfloss type of cake again), he proudly showed us his church. He was particularly keen to show us his efforts at inculturation and the two tabernacles – one for the Eucharist and one for the Scriptures – which were mounted on the wall behind the altar. The bishop expressed the opinion that the most significant development in the Church in recent years was the realisation that the Christian message had to be expressed and lived out in the culture of the country in which it was living and growing.

We didn't realise that we all – the bishop and his chaplain, Francis, Cathy and I – were to go out for a Chinese meal afterwards. But by this time Cathy and I were using the phrase 'go with the flow', because repeatedly things happened that we had not been told about. The illuminated sign outside said it was a Chinese restaurant, but we saw nothing particularly 'Chinese' about it. The waiters and cooks, we were told, were all locals. Cathy and I sat either side of the bishop. He was definitely rather traditional and most uncomfortable about discussing married priests and other modern issues; he was, however, very fluent on the subject of inculturation. Back at our Caritas base we got on with our report writing and at 10pm I went off to bed to write up this diary entry. Another full and fascinating day.

Reflection

In this developing nation, which has never experienced an industrial revolution as we have in Europe, all work is very labour intensive and markets are as they must have been for hundreds of years. Jesus would certainly be more at home in their market place than in our supermarkets.

Advent reflection

John the Baptist, like Khan Jahan, was a holy man who directed the people's thoughts away from the ordinary of the market place, with all its buying and selling, to the silent and spiritual which gives real meaning and purpose to life. 'Repent' is the familiar call of the prophet or holy man; a call and a challenge to each of us. The call is directed to me, not to my friend, partner or colleague at work; to me.

Scripture text

John said to the crowds coming out to be baptised by him, 'You brood of vipers! Who warned you to flee from the coming wrath? Produce fruit in keeping with repentance.' *Luke 3:7*

Prayer

Ever loving and forgiving Father,
    help me to accept that I do wrong;
    that I fall short of Christ's expectations of me;
    that I sin.
To have a change of heart and truly repent,
I must start by accepting that I have failed.
Help me to be truly sorry
    and make a genuine effort to do better.
Without your help I cannot succeed;
    but with you helping me
    all things are possible. Amen

DAY EIGHT

Losing everything but dignity

It was a very humid night and I did not sleep at all well. No traffic to wake you here – beautiful bird song instead. There are lots and lots of rickshaws in Khulna town, but here all is quiet and peaceful. The compound covers an acre and there are offices as well as the guest-house accommodation for visitors who come for the regular courses. There is also a large pond with fish in it, and very noisy rooks in the surrounding trees. Francis said that many Bengalis who come on the courses prefer to come down to wash and shower in the pond rather than use the cold shower provided in the room.

Reviewing how I'm coping, I seem to be in a 'receiving' or an 'accepting' mode. What I mean is, I'm finding it difficult to think or reflect and, also, to pray; probably because it is still such a culture shock.

Early start again through the rickshaw-thronged streets for a one-and-a-half-hour drive through the countryside – so many small lakes and ponds – to Satkhira and the flooded region. It was a disturbing sight! A month after the flooding and the water level had dropped by about a metre, with still another metre or more standing there. Water for as far as we could see on either side of the road. Along the roadside, mile after mile, were the tiny huts (homes) of the displaced families.

At Satkhira we visited the local Caritas office and got an update on the situation. No one, it seems, knows when the water level will drop or how to get it to go down! They've tried breaking through dykes but that caused fighting between different groups. This local office is the home of the IWDP (Independent Women's Development Programme). We were greeted with bouquets of flowers by the women co-ordinators of the programme, all looking so colourful in their bright saris. At the usual type of meeting – after the customary introductions – we learnt about their work. They form groups of women (about 335 groups in this area) who save money regularly then, with approval of the group, borrow credit for small businesses. The groups are also used for educational purposes, and the development of various skills.

On the way we had stopped at the roadside because we were in a sugar-cane growing area and had noticed that it was being harvested and pulped. It was a really picturesque scene and they were using basic agricultural technology. The working group of men and women were producing Gur, a type of sweet similar to fudge. A belt-driven crusher extracted the juice from the cane which was collected and boiled (Cathy, who knows about these things, told me it was a 'rolling' boil). The juice was boiled in two separate operations and then poured into small moulds. The whole enterprise was taking place in the open air with just a simple canopy over the boiling operation to protect the workers from the sun.)

Further up the road we witnessed more flood destruction and many more displaced people – half a million lost their homes. We stopped at a little encampment and a small crowd gathered – we were immediately besieged by curious adults and children as we wandered into it. I felt really embarrassed; here were we, with our stylish western clothes and hi-tech cameras, getting out of a high-powered vehicle to stare at those who had nothing and had lost even that! (Mind you, they were doing more staring than we were.) We interviewed a young mother who was sitting on a rush mat in a shelter which was a cube, 6ft by 6ft by 6ft, with no observable possessions. She told us that her name was Puspa Balydangi. Snuggled up to her was Madori, her two-and-a-half-year-old daughter (it was hard to tell the child was a girl, because her head was shaved). I didn't like the idea of standing and looking down on her, so I sat on the mat just outside the 'shelter', in the blazing sun, with no hat on. Puspa told us that she had two other children of school age and her husband had gone to find fodder for their two cows which they had been able to rescue. The waters had come pouring in, early in the morning, at 3am and they had been taken completely by surprise as there had been no flooding in their district for 60 years or more.

They had, so far, been a month in these shelters and had no idea how long it would take before they could go back and start again. Very touchingly Puspa got concerned about me sitting out in the sun and moved over to make space for me in the shade of the shelter. I declined, saying that we were about to leave. (I felt that this was an experience that I would never forget.) After we had left Puspa we met the local Catholic priest, Father Albino, who has been working with the displaced people. I told him of Puspa's concern; how she who had lost everything but had never complained was only concerned about me suffering from the sun! He wasn't surprised, saying that it was very typical of these people who were generously supporting and helping one another. It had been a typical generous gesture.

We walked a little way up the road, to a point where the Red Crescent (the equivalent to the Red Cross in an Islamic country) was giving out parcels of food. Many people, mainly women and children, were lined up, standing patiently and waiting their turn. A bundle made of sacking and containing 5 kilos of rice and some lentils was being given to each family – to last two days. The Red Crescent workers were very keen to tell us how they were volunteers and show us what they were doing. However, we didn't stop long because it was clear that we were in the way – blocking an entrance and an exit.

Nearby there was an army post. We stopped the car to get out to talk to the young corporal; almost immediately an officer, adjusting his uniform as he came, appeared on the scene. They had little to tell us except that they had used the motorboats we could see drawn up at the water's edge, on the roadside, to rescue a lot of people.

Lunch was at Fr Albino's house which was part of a compound, including a church and an orphanage for 100 boys. We were thoughtfully given a room each for an hour's siesta. (The bed was very hard with no mattress.) Afterwards we crossed the road to visit Sister Raphaela and her sisters who run an orphanage for 50 girls. We received the usual kind hospitality and were told that the girls, 6-11 years of age, were studying. (All the local schools were closed because of the flooding, so they were working 'at home'.) Outside, after our chat with Sister Raphaela, they were released from their study and swarmed around us, wanting to hold our hands. I had four girls clinging to each hand! There was lots of laughter and several photos were taken. It was quite an emotional experience – the girls so desperately wanted attention and love. With great difficulty, and reluctance, we detached ourselves and left, but not before leaving one of our carrier bags full of 'goodies' (colouring pencils, books, little purses, etc.) with them. We were all impressed by Sister Raphaela's total dedication to the girls. She had been a high school headteacher before 'retiring' to take up this work (she must have been about 70 years of age).

On the return journey we made an unscheduled stop at a roadside potter's business. A big man of about 50, he invited us into his yard and his open-sided workshop. Dullchander Pal expertly and swiftly 'threw' two pots for us. I was surprised by the huge wheel he was using – the size of a small tractor tyre. He first spun it by standing over it and using a stick to get it revolving very fast. Then he sat down and worked the clay. The wheel required no more attention until he needed it for a second pot. He told us that business for potters was declining.

There had been many potters in the area but he, and one other, were the only ones who remained. Plastic goods were killing his trade. We told him that the beautiful pots he made would sell at a great profit in English garden centres. He told us that he had no way of exporting them. His wife and family were part of the enterprise and finished off his work. An elder daughter of about 20 gave us each a gift of a pottery money 'box'. We continued to see flooded areas as we drove back to Khulna.

Reflection

Out of all the many memorable sights and sounds of the day, the chat with Puspa in her little shelter and her concern for me sitting in the sun will always be an enduring memory. She, who had lost everything, was worried about a passing wealthy western visitor! If only I could daily show as much concern for others.

Advent reflection

Puspa reminded me of Mary, the humble and patient young woman from Nazareth, who could do nothing but wait – as all expectant mothers have to uncomfortably wait – for the outcome of Gabriel's message and its meaning. What did she do when she heard her cousin was pregnant? She rushed off to help! I would not be surprised if Mary, on arrival in Bethlehem, was more worried about other fellow-travellers than herself. More concerned that others got shelter for the night than about her own imminent labour. Being more aware of others' needs than our own, would prepare us well for God's unselfish gift of himself to us.

Scripture text

Mary set out at that time
and went as quickly as she could
  to a town in the hill country
  of Judah.
Luke 1:39

Prayer

I am often ungrateful, Lord, often unappreciative
  of what you have done for me, and of what others do.
May this Christmas find me keen to express my thanks
  to all those around me who have shown me
  love and kindness this year.
May this Christmas find me more prepared
  to put the concerns and cares of others,
  before my own selfish interests. Amen

DAY NINE

The generous poor

Stephen gave me a large free-standing fan from his room to use all night in my rather airless room. So it was a more comfortable night and I slept better. I wondered if I was drinking enough water, but then there was the problem of continual long car journeys and I didn't want to be stopping the car!

What a day this has been! It started with a meeting in an attractive lecture hall, of all the field workers of the Caritas Regional office (this was the first day of their working week). There were introductions on both sides – garlands of flowers were put round our necks and we were given gifts – hand-carved wall plaques of Bangladesh country scenes – wrapped in blue 'birthday' gift-wrapping.

After a longish drive and more and more rural scenes we arrived at the Dumuria Caritas rural office. The all-male staff welcomed us with bouquets of the slender white flower – rajani gandha ('night scent') – and the usual introductions. We learnt about the six development projects funded and overseen from there; then we went out to see three examples, all funded by loans from Caritas. Before we left I had a 'go' on a rower pump outside the office. As I was pulling the handle towards me – and so releasing the water – one of the field workers, an educated man, asked me in English, 'Do you have pumps like this in your country?' He was surprised and even concerned when I said 'No'. I added that every house had its own water supply and tap. 'Every house?' he asked, with real surprise.

The first example of a successful loan project was a plant nursery. At Sajeara we met Mohammed Zakir Hussain (28) the proprietor of a nursery of mahogany and teak trees. He started with just the loan, but now employs 10 casual workers (all members of his extended family); with further loans he has expanded his activities to include a fishpond; and his latest project is a shed for 500 chickens, which is to be completed. We could not believe our eyes when his men went into the pond dressed as they were, with fishing nets. The water was above their waists and they came out with gigantic prawns – about 9 inches long – looking more like small lobsters.

From there it was a 15-minute drive to Sahapur to visit a family whose 20-year-old son had borrowed money to develop a pond behind his family home. It was a lovely setting, if a bit wet (I fell in the mud). A simple rural scene, with all manner of animals sharing the area behind the house with the family, who, with their friends, all crowded round to view the visitors. We sat on the rough and obligatory chairs set out under the trees close to the pond. Cathy was a great hit with the women who took her off to the house. Jafar Islam (the 20-year-old) told us about his plans to extend the roof – their home had a bit of a shop fronting the road – to keep 200 chickens up there! He insisted on showing us his accounts for the last three years and they revealed quite a handsome profit. We had a happy photo with the family.

Then we made a short, but perilous journey down a tortuous brick-laid, very uneven and narrow road. (Several times the driver had to stop, get out and check if the vehicle could get across gaps and holes or round the bony cows who insisted on lying in the road.) The following experience was a 'knock-out': we dismounted and walked into a small community area of mud houses and there were 24 women in bright saris waiting for us. They were sitting cross-legged in a horseshoe or rough square, with the chairwoman sitting in the middle. On the open side were four chairs. I asked if we could sit, like the women, on the matting. So we took off our sandals and did that.

This group is called Adarsha Mohila Samity (ideal women's group). They introduced themselves and then we did the same. We asked them questions – lots of laughter – and they asked us questions. In response to one of our questions, a spinning wheel to spin coconut thread was produced and skilfully demonstrated. Their simple, innocent questions revealed that they had not the slightest idea of life in England. 'What are your houses like? Are they like ours, made of mud?' 'Is life a struggle for you, like it is for us?' 'Are the people religious in your country?' The group met regularly not only for savings/loans (some women were into their third loan, over a period of seven years) but also for education and instruction on sanitation and hygiene. (There was a visual aid hanging from a tree at the front of the group.) The chairwoman presented Cathy with her most precious possession – a large papaya fruit from her tree. We could happily have stayed much longer talking to these confident, cheerful – but struggling – women; but we moved on.

The next experience nearly blew my mind! After a fairly short journey we arrived one hour late at the Chuknagorc school. A long shed-like building for the poorest of the Hindu people, the untouchables. This was one of several Hindu communities in this part of Bangladesh, not too far from the borders of India. When we got out of the car there was a beautiful decorated arch saying 'Welcome' and the children were drawn up in six lines, one behind the other. Three bigger girls in saris came forward and gave us a Hindu ceremonial welcome with dance, marking our foreheads with a yellow sandalwood liquid and sprinkling us with little flowers and petals. This was followed by some 'drill' by the children who received orders from a young girl of about 10. (She would make a brilliant sergeant-major!) Inside there were more bouquets, a silver bangle tied to our right wrists and kisses from young 8-9-year-old girls. This was followed by dance and song. Two graduates of about 24 delivered two prepared speeches in English. One young woman, Ratna Das, told us that their village had 500 persons, most of whom were Hindu, and they were very indebted to Caritas and the Catholic Fathers 'for help in so many ways'. (She gave us a copy of the speech, which I have.) Both graduates had been students of this rudimentary school. This was followed by a role-play about child brides. There was a lot of music and laughter, and a volume of chatter from the younger children at the back of the school building. It was a truly memorable occasion.

We had not eaten since breakfast and it was now 4pm. We drove to the local Caritas regional office for some 'lunch'. On our return to Khulna we went to evening Mass at the cathedral. There were no pews, just matting; the women were sitting or standing on the right side (facing the altar) and the men on the left. Naturally it was in Bangla, but the structure was the same and the music was lively. Afterwards we had coffee with the parish priest in his house.

At 7pm, after a wash and brush-up, we were collected by the director of NGO Forum and taken to their offices for a briefing. It included the usual introductions and a presentation on WATSAN (water and sanitation projects), preparing us for what we are going to see, so we are told, tomorrow. Their team then took us to a convivial meal at a Chinese restaurant (although again it wasn't very Chinese).

It is now 10.30pm and we have to be up early for a 7am departure (we are really being worked hard).

Reflection

The poor give so generously. How narrow minded and mistaken we are to imagine that only Christians are generous in giving. The Hindu poor today could not have made us more welcome; and the Muslim groups too have shown such love. For me it contrasts starkly with a visit I made on a hot summer's day to a Catholic religious house in London where I was not even offered a drink of water!

Advent reflection

Poverty unites people. When you have very little, or nothing, you understand poverty and the needs others have. You understand generosity and dependence upon God. Mary and Joseph were poor; and Mary was pregnant. It was undoubtedly some poor person who pointed out the stable – an unexpected luxury for a couple who expected to spend their night on the streets. The baby born that night was to say, later in life, 'How hard it is for the rich to enter the kingdom of heaven.' And we are the rich!

Scripture text

You have been a refuge for the poor,
  a refuge for the needy in his distress,
  a shelter from the storm and a shade from the heat.
Isaiah 25:4

Prayer

Almighty God and Father of all,
  rich and poor,
  when your Son became a human being,
  like us in all things, except sin,
  he came as a member of a poor family.
Help us, who live in comfort,
  to have poverty of heart
  that we may enter into union
  with those who know real poverty.
May our generous love for them
  bring us into closer union with you. Amen

DAY TEN

Safe water for life

Greeted by the dawn chorus at 6am. It had been a long and disturbed night. My dry cough (result of Dhaka pollution?) seemed to be made worse by the fan so, during one of my several 'wanderings around' the room in the night, I switched it off. The heat was better than the fan, but I still didn't sleep. As I've probably written before, the trouble is we are bombarded with sensory, emotional and cultural experiences all day long, then we concentrate on compiling a report and follow that with writing this diary. There's no opportunity to unwind before bedtime. Still, I'm sure I shall survive!

We left with the NGO Forum gentleman for an inspection of their water projects.

Another 14-hour day – very tiring but a very rewarding experience. We drove for about an hour and a half, crossed two rivers on ferries, and then we stopped at a riverside village where we took an engine boat (a simple wooden boat with a very noisy engine) across a wide river and up a tributary. It was difficult to enter because the mouth of the tributary was choked with floating water-lily plants which were pretty but not easy to navigate (they'd gone when we returned). We arrived to the usual warm welcome at the Morelgong regional office – presented with more flowers, and introductions all round. We sat outside the actual office in a beautiful circular arbour, with sightseers (mainly children) looking on.

The field officers explained their WATSAN (water and sanitation) programme and we inspected some latrines, of various styles, under construction. Accompanied by two confident young women teachers, Mansura and Parvin (who help to deliver informal education of three-hour sessions a day in the villages), we set out on an hour-long 'voyage' up this very wide river. (There were so many interesting sights to see that I felt frustrated at not having enough film with me to indulge my desire to 'shoot' everything. On the journey my personal photo album went round the boat. Mohammed Hussain, the programme organiser who has a master's degree in sociology said, 'Tony, you are a very wealthy man', as he pointed to a picture of my semi-detached home. I tried to explain that I wasn't – but certainly to him, in the setting of his country, I am.

We arrived eventually at the Bohorbunia village on the banks of the river. There was no jetty or docking – you just leapt for the bank and hoped for the best! We were led through to a simple courtyard between the mud houses where a meeting was in progress. The chairperson and his deputy were retired headteachers and the local doctor was also sitting cross-legged in the group among the group members. The men sat on one side of this square and the women, Moslem and Hindu together, sat opposite. The chairpersons, using visual displays on rough poles, were on the third side and we, the visitors, opposite them. (We declined chairs and sat like everyone else on the matting.) More introductions . . . more bouquets of flowers. We were told what they were planning about sanitation and a safe water supply. Attractive young women pressed loads of food on us! (We learnt later that many of the villagers found us interesting, because they had never seen a white person before.)

One of the retired headteachers wanted to talk to me about literature . . . Mohammed Hussain wanted to talk about Tony Blair and the Labour Party and asked my opinion about the English Poor Laws of 1860 (did I get the date right?). It was such a contrast: down single tracks, negotiating very muddy streams over tiny rocking bamboo 'bridges', while holding a serious conversation with one or other of the educated men! They were a brilliant group of people, living there in the forest by the river. They told us how the Moslems and Hindus share in one another's religious festivals and generally support one another. We avoided answering questions about our own economic situation because the truth would have been too embarrassing to relate! At the end a wonderful, almost toothless old lady dressed in a black sari said with a twinkle in her eye, 'God sends us many trials, but we must be thankful, because he also sent us you!' (We were humbled at every turn.)

A little further down the riverbank we arrived at another part of the same village which has three parts. Here a young woman teacher was instructing women with some visual aids, including a *white* doll which could be wound up to crawl, and a toy parrot! This lesson too was about sanitation. Again we sat in the group, introduced ourselves and asked and answered questions.

A big lunch followed at the retired headteacher's mud home – the usual rice, fish and delicious great big prawns! We then moved to the third part of the village where a drama group, including the two young teachers who had accompanied us, were putting on a series of short educational plays on an open-air stage. It was a picturesque scene. There was a large audience of village people of all ages who were really caught up in the action of the drama which was about using proper toilets, safe water, getting ripped off by the local landlord, etc. (although we couldn't follow the dialogue the gestures and actions made the message very clear all the time). More fond farewells – they are such patient, gentle and cheerful people.

Back on to the engine boat and off to another village further up the river where there was a meeting of pump caretakers in progress. It was a strict Moslem village and a bright canopy had been erected over the meeting to stop outsiders from seeing the women in the group. Their pump is painted red on the front pipe because they have an arsenic problem! It has to be tested regularly with a kit provided by CAFOD and they showed us how it is done.

After the long journey back, during which we witnessed an incident when a group of teenage lads refused to pay a ferry charge, we had dinner at the NGO Forum's offices. Then we got back to report writing at 9.30pm and late to bed again.

Reflection

This was a day centred around 'water' and it brought home to me how we in the West take 'safe' water for granted. These experiences make so clear what a vast economic gulf exists between the ordinary people (I suppose I count myself as ordinary) of the western wealthy world and the ordinary people of the struggling, developing, countries. How truly blessed with safe water, electricity and material prosperity we are; and we just do not realise or appreciate it.

Advent reflection

'Water' and Advent bring John the Baptist to mind. He heralds a new order which can only come in and find acceptance if people first repent of their old ways. A sign of this 'new life' is immersion in water. Although we have been baptised it does not absolve us of the need to repent and be aware that we constantly need to seek forgiveness and start afresh. John the Baptist makes material demands of his hearers; these could be the starting point for an Advent meditation.

Scripture text

'What should we do then?' the crowd asked. John answered, 'The man with two tunics should share with him who has none, and the one who has food should do the same.' *Luke 3:10-11*

Prayer

Patient and loving Father,
    why are we so impatient and so unappreciative?
We always seem to be harassed and under pressure
    and everyone speaks of being stressed.

Yet, we have all the important ingredients
  for a happy, comfortable life.
Our water supply is safe and food is plentiful.
Our homes are packed with labour-saving devices
  and machines for leisure-filled entertainment;
  and yet we are still not happy!
Perhaps if we repented of our ingratitude,
  and our lack of concern for the poor,
  we might find peace – a peace this hectic world
  cannot give.
May we learn, this Advent,
  appreciation for all your gifts. Amen

Forest meetings

After a better night we were out by 7am on the road to the Sundarban forest. (I have learnt one Bangla word, *Dhanyabad*, which means 'thank you'; we need it all the time because everyone is so generous with their time and efforts for us.) At nearly every stop we were offered green coconut milk, either in a glass or in the coconut itself (they cut the top off with a machete and put a straw in for drinking). After a hair-raising drive along narrow roads with animals and humans scurrying out of our path as we honked our way at speed, we came to the river and boarded an engine boat. We proceeded south, down river, with sights on both banks but little river traffic. Apparently permits had to be obtained for us to enter the forest and two guards with rather antique-looking rifles were provided. Our guide joked that there were two just in case one rifle didn't work! We had to be prepared in case we met 'uncle', the Bengal tiger, who roamed these forests.

We had collected the guards from the Forestry Protection Office, where we saw loads of wood from the forest that had been confiscated. (We heard it said later that the forestry officers are some of the worst for accepting bribes.) After fifteen minutes we came into the bank and moored. It wasn't a proper landing place and we clambered out into the forest (the armed guards went first). I was immediately struck by how thick the undergrowth was and how wet and muddy the soil. After five minutes of pushing aside branches, etc., we paused; I noticed some tracks, with clear paw marks. I asked what they were and the guide/interpreter told us that they were tiger tracks. We also saw tracks of deer and jackal.

We returned the armed guard to the forestry station and collected the officer in charge. We noticed that the trees along the path and approach to the forestry station had been painted with red and white stripes. We asked why and were told, 'In honour of your visit!' With the officer on board we set off down river and moored at the forest edge for a picnic lunch. On this occasion, for the first time, I refused cutlery and copied our companions, eating with my right hand.

After returning the officer to his station we proceeded further up the river and moored again. We walked along a narrow path, over rickety, narrow little bamboo bridges and shortly we came to a very poor village. Sixteen women were waiting for us in their colourful saris, gold studs in their noses. A young woman in a blue sari led this group. After learning about their group, we exchanged questions. They wanted advice about what to do when men were paid 60 taka for a day's work and women got 25 for the same work! Cathy gave them some ideas and we pointed out that in our country there had been a similar problem, with women getting less pay for the same work. We noticed that it was a mixed group of ten Muslim and six Hindu women. 'How can we come out of poverty?' was a hard question for us.

They are more aware, they said, of signs of hope for the future. Some of them were honey-gatherers working in the forest and their husbands worked in the forest as tree-fellers, etc. They said that they were learning how the forest must be protected. A Prodipon (NGO) worker lived among them and gave them help and guidance. They had hopes that their children would be able to go to school and have a better life. 'Yes, life was a little better and there's more joy in life these days!' one answered. They were so delighted that we had come to see them and said how encouraging it was for them.

The return seemed a long journey in the noisy engine boat. Back at 6pm, we were out again an hour later and treated to dinner at 'Castle Salim', another 'Chinese' restaurant. Asked about the problem of trafficking in women and children, our host said that he thought about 500 women and children a month were disappearing, taken across into India, for spare-part surgery, prostitution, etc. He told us that an 11-year-old daughter of one of the women we had met that day had been abducted the week before. She had been offered a flower by an attractively dressed woman, sniffed it, and came round in a hut, tied up with other children. Thankfully they got free and escaped.

It has been another exciting day, including seeing a dolphin in the river and two sea eagles.

Reflection

I'm feeling more and more disturbed about roaring around the country lanes (their major roads) scattering young goats, ducks, chickens and humans helter-skelter in a super Toyota Spacecruiser. It even plays a melody from Beethoven as it reverses! The Europeans sweep into town, make a few gracious visits – like royalty – say a few bland things and then are whisked away again in air-conditioned splendour, allowing the gaping crowd to return to their daily struggle!

Advent reflection

What did Joseph think of the smart houses of the rich Sadducee families on the outskirts of Jerusalem, which the couple had to pass to reach

Bethlehem? Did he, as a rough Galilean, pass any comment about the idleness of the wealthy and the opulence of the priestly community? How surprised he would be to know that some 30 years later his foster son would say, 'Blessed are the poor, the kingdom of heaven is theirs.'

Scripture text

The Sovereign Lord has filled me with his Spirit.
He has chosen me and sent me
   to bring good news to the poor,
   to heal the broken-hearted,
   to announce release to captives
   and freedom to those in prison.'
Isaiah 61:1

Prayer

Lord, the human race never expected
   the gift of your very self
   in the person of your Son;
   a Messiah, yes,
   but your very self, no!
An equal surprise
   was your identification with the poor,
   when riches were thought to be
   a sign of God's favour.
May I learn from your amazing gift,
   and be generous of heart.
May I learn from your love of the poor,
   and reveal the same love in my life. Amen

DAY TWELVE

A day for reflection

Our first break and opportunity to reflect and write our reports. Getting accustomed now to mosquito nets, ear plugs and a cold-water shower and shave. Breakfast at 8am and at 9 we settled down to report writing. It was a relaxing and peaceful morning, an opportunity to gather a few thoughts and share a few insights and impressions. At noon we went to the 'town' to find an office/shop that provides phone facilities. On the third attempt I got through to home, where it was 6.15am, and spoke to Louise, Liz and Tom. They spoke of the terrible flooding back home and reported that they had only received one of my e-mails.

We were even allowed a siesta today! Later we went back to town to a parade of small shops – the nearest thing to European shops that we had seen. Cathy bought a couple of outfits, one a beautiful 'mirror' sari with lots of tiny 'mirrors' sewn into the design. I only spent 30 taka (40p) on a wedding mat for the 'Islam artefacts' box at school. We then drove to the agricultural/engineering university just outside Khulna. We had been invited to a 'freshers' (new intake) ceremony, but they were not ready and we spent the best part of an hour talking to various professors in the office of the faculty head. (As we entered his office at 4.30pm he was on his knees on his prayer mat, just inside the door.) He proved to be a very lively and jovial man who had studied for his degree at Sheffield, England, and his English was perfect. We never saw the ceremony because we had a dinner date to prepare for.

Back at the Caritas compound we freshened up and went out to dinner with the local vicar-general, Father James. He was lively and charming and had three other young priests with him. I passed a comment about the energetic and handsome young priests we had met, in comparison to the mainly elderly and ageing priests back home. After a 'Tiger' beer – not generally permitted elsewhere in this country, but brought in by an Italian priest, we were told – we enjoyed a good meal. It was the usual menu, but with the addition of cheese and biscuits and coffee. The conversation and conviviality flowed. (All the priests were in open-necked shirts; we haven't seen any in 'clerical' attire yet.) On the way back at 9.15pm the streets were as busy as earlier in the day: all the 'shops' and workshops still busy – ironworkers welding on the pavement, weavers weaving on the pavement – all in their small roadside units. Francis, our guide, told us that it starts to close down at about 10pm and opens up again at 5am!

(Everywhere we've been we've seen people work, work, working.) I saw one cinema – not used much, Francis said – with garish posters, and one petrol station with one pump, and *that* was idle! Francis estimated that 70 per cent of homes had no electricity and those that had it could not rely on it, as we had witnessed. So there's not much point in having a fridge, even if you could afford it. I have seen no bars here as I had in Dhaka, with a black-and-white TV and men crowding round watching.

We leave Khulna tomorrow morning at 8am for the 330-kilometre drive to Dhaka. It will probably take seven hours, but it will depend upon the ferries.

Reflection

Every time we come up to the iron gates of the Caritas compound with its large Caritas emblem – Caritas means love – the driver honks the horn for the gateman to let us in. As we wait in the road I look guiltily at the slum dwellings and one-room huts opposite the gates, with the poor people sitting out under the street light, on the actual road. They sit in utter destitution opposite the word 'Caritas'. My conscience prompted me to ask one of the Caritas directors about this; he said, 'They haven't asked for any help'!

Advent reflection

Are my eyes and my heart really open to those with whom I work and live? Or do I live such a self-contained, fretful existence that I am totally caught up in *my* concerns, *my* interests? That's hardly what Christ would expect of us. It certainly isn't in the spirit of Advent, which is our 'waiting upon' the appearing of the Son of God; the Father's unselfish gift to us.

Scripture text

See, a king will reign in righteousness . . .
Then the eyes of those who see will no longer be closed,
    and the ears of those who hear will listen.
Isaiah 32:1, 3

Prayer

Lord of generous self-giving,
    open my eyes and my heart
    to those in need around me.
May I not be blinded
    by my own selfish needs
    but see you in all. Amen

Return to Dhaka

Here we are back in Dhaka, with its pollution, after an eight-hour journey. It is 4.30pm as I write and a mullah is blasting away on a powerful PA system; I assume they are Islamic phrases and songs. Oh, for the peace of Khulna! It was a long drive and although Cathy didn't like it, invaluable; to drive through the countryside and see so many sights that I will never see again. For example: the fields being ploughed with two oxen and a wooden plough; in one place three ploughs were working one field. We only saw two tractors – old red things – and no other form of mechanisation. We drove for mile after mile without seeing a private car, but the roads were very busy with the decorated heavy lorries (the kings of the road, in their minds and reluctant to abandon the centre of the road). On the rusting ancient ferry, after a rough and ready approach to it, we saw two customs officers argue with two young men. They took their heavy load from the top of a bus, down the side of the ferry into a tiny rowing boat which they commandeered, and across to the shore. 'Probably smuggling,' Francis commented.

The crossing of the Ganges (known as the Padmar River in Bangladesh) was on this large bus-and-lorry-carrying ferry, with an interesting collection of pedestrians, hawkers, sellers of snacks, etc. I saw a boatload of cows sailing past and couldn't resist a photo. Nearer to Dhaka there were many open-back lorries with cows standing jammed in the back (animal-rights activists in England would have gone berserk!). At Jessore, to break the journey, we stopped at a Catechetical Centre – a beautiful place with lovely grounds – for a coffee and a chat with Sister Bruno, an American Holy Cross sister who has been in Bangladesh for more than 40 years. She told us that they took in 1,000 people during the recent flooding, and allowed them to camp in their grounds.

On our return we met up again with Chris, Steve and Anne-Marie; exchanged stories and experiences.

The mullah outside (10.30pm) is *still* going strong. We escaped for a couple of hours down to the Sheraton hotel where we had a beer. We must be up at 6.30am tomorrow for another early start.

Reflection

It seemed and felt wrong to 'take time out' at the Sheraton Hotel, after all the poverty we have seen. On the other hand we are of a different culture which is accustomed to leisure time and all we are seeing is stressful for us. A drink and a laugh together help you to cope.

Advent reflection

Liturgical tradition keeps the third Sunday of Advent as *Gaudate Sunday* when pink vestments may be worn. When, in earlier times, Advent was a season of fasting the Church thought it important to give people a break, just for one day, from the rigours of Advent. A good concept, for we cannot humanly take too much unrelieved pressure or deprivation. But have we spiritually done enough this Advent to merit a break? What has happened to our Advent resolutions? Have we been trying to keep them?

Scripture text

Give strength to hands that are tired and to knees that tremble with weakness. Tell everyone who is discouraged, 'Be strong and don't be afraid! God is coming to your rescue.'
Isaiah 35:3-4

Prayer

Father Creator, you created us,
   not to 'have a good time',
   but to know, love and serve you
   and thereby find happiness.
While we need leisure time,
   and you truly want us to be happy,
   may our target be the happiness
   of others and their well-being.
Let us leave the bestowing of joy
   as a gift that we hope to receive from you. Amen

DAY FOURTEEN

Down into the slums

The first ever Bangladesh Test Match begins today, against India; hopes are high, but expectations are not! Out at 8.15am – the car was late arriving for us. It was provided by the National Federation of Garment Workers (Caritas would not provide us with a car to make this visit!). We were told that we were meeting some garment workers this morning; I don't know quite what I was expecting, but I wasn't prepared for the reality. We were taken to the slums of Dhaka – a type of shanty town built on rickety stilts above a dreadful, smelly rubbish tip! I've felt secure the whole of this visit, until now. I lost my bearings, there was nothing to relate to; it was all new and distressing and so I felt out of my depth; it was really a little frightening. We've seen rural poverty, but this was something else! Here we saw, smelt and felt it. Words fail. It was a stomach-turning, heart-wrenching experience that I shall never forget.

We first went down some filthy lanes with thin, staring folk working, selling or just sitting; then onto a rickety bamboo walkway, about 8 feet above an evil-looking, smelly tip full of rotting rubbish. (An area that floods in the rainy season.) Next down a very narrow walkway passage, passing 'rooms' that were people's homes. We climbed up and into one family's home which measured about 15ft by 15ft. We sat on the large 'platform' which was, presumably, where people slept; that filled about one-third of the room. People, especially young women, crowded in. The official from the Federation acted as interpreter. We listened intently to the stories of the young workers. There was Asma, 14 years of age, who works as a 'helper' and earns 600 taka a month – 9 hours a day for 7 days a week (about £8 a month). Zulekaza (16) a machinist who turns out 60 shirt collars an hour and earns 1,500 taka a month (about £20).

From this home we went on, along another walkway above the rubbish tip, to another 'room'; this was in a block with communal washing facilities (which were being used by some men) just a few feet away opposite the 'home' we entered. Again we sat on a blue-and-white covered platform or 'bed' and gazed in wonder at the pots and few possessions stacked around the walls on shelves and on a few pieces of furniture. (An English dictionary lay on a shelf beside where I sat, alongside an exam paper for English.) Here we met Rahuma (15) who has been working in a garment factory since she was 9 years of age. She had started at 600 taka, but was now earning 1,500 taka a month. Her family live in Mymensingh. They had sent her to Dhaka when she was 9 to find a job as they could not afford to support her; she has four sisters and two brothers! Her day starts at 7.15am for the walk to work which begins at 8am. She should finish at 5pm, but regularly has to work until 10pm; sometimes all night on rush jobs. She then has to walk home, eat, sleep and so on to another day. Sometimes they get Friday off and sometimes not.

We heard several similar stories. One of the girls (I think I should omit her name) told us about the two lists that the factories operate. The garment workers have to sign both lists each month. The first list states that they have been paid 930 taka a month – the minimum legal wage for a helper – and that they had Friday off. The second list shows the actual money received – 600 taka for the month, and the true hours worked. The first list is for the inspection of any Government official or any foreign buyer who asks if the workers are being paid properly! (Should I write to the buyers when I get home?)

We trod carefully over the bamboo 'bridge' on our exit and returned to the litter-strewn lanes. An old man was sitting by the roadside, 'tattooing' (stamping with a dye) the hands of passers-by who were prepared to part with a taka for the service. We stopped and Cathy had her hand stamped; the old man at first refused payment until it was pressed on him.

We next went to visit a factory where the production manager was a friend of the Federation chairman who was with us, and sympathetic to the union (unusual). He had started out as a cutter in the same factory and made his way up to production manager. Before the visit we had been cautioned about asking too many searching questions, but he appeared to be open, telling us how the factory worked and about pay and conditions. On the stairs up to his office, clearly on view, was a Code of Conduct. He was happy that it was being implemented, e.g. sufficient fire exits, extinguishers, meal breaks and overtime payments being made on time. On a tour of the factory we saw the machinists working furiously, with their helpers. We saw the quality control people and the finishers. It was very noisy and people were working very close together, but it wasn't as bad as I thought it was going to be. (However, we learnt later that this was a Class A factory, in other words, the very best.) They were fulfilling a shirt order for Canada (shirts labelled at $9.99).

We visited a second factory, very similar to the first; the production manager was older but very lively and confident. We asked about the age of two machinists, who looked about 12. He said they were 18, they just looked young! He took us upstairs to where an extension was being built; half of the area, he said, would be a canteen where the workers could eat. Both managers thought that they could fight off competition from China.

The first supplied Wal-Mart (owners of Asda), the second was working on an order for Germany. We called in on the office of the National Federation of Garment Workers – a coalhole of a place – tucked down more squalid back alleys.

As the car had gone without us, we returned to Caritas by 'baby taxi' (another new experience). Collected from Caritas, after lunch, we returned to the Union 'office' for a meeting with union members, who were all rather young (compared to me). The Federation tries to encourage trade unions in the factories – which are perfectly legal – but the factory owners won't allow them and sack any known members. (A young man told us how he had recently lost his job because he had started a union.) All those present, of 14 years and upwards, were secret members of a union. They are currently campaigning for one day off a week! This is required by law, but none of the factory owners pay any attention.

The Union has been fighting for compensation for the victims of fires in factories (193 workers have died in separate fires since December 1999). The problems for workers from the floods were highlighted. If a factory is closed because of flooding – or they can't get the goods in and out – there is no work; no work means no pay, no pay means no food! There was an exchange of questions and answers.

The small room was jam-packed with interested people. We interviewed Amena as a contrast to a British girl aged 15. She stood nervously by her friends as we asked her questions about her life. (It was a similar story to what we had heard in the slums.) She has been a garment worker since the age of 11. Now she operates a sewing machine, making shirts and trousers; she earns 1,500 taka a month (£20). Her day begins at 5am; she washes, cooks and then walks 5 kilometres to start work at 8am. She has one break for a meal in the middle of the day which she eats on the roof as there is no canteen. She works until 5pm, but sometimes until 10 pm; occasionally all night to 4am. (In other words, from 8am to 4am!) Whatever time she stops, she has to be back at work by 8am. She might get Friday off – she did today – but that is not assured.

Back at the Caritas offices a team of people had arrived from other Asian countries for an international meeting. We sat and wrote up our reports until 10.30pm – another long but incredibly interesting day. We are going to be allowed to lie in until 7.30am tomorrow!

Reflection

Today we came face to face with real poverty, the result of greed. The greed of the factory owners who want to maximise profits; the greed of the big clothing companies who sell to our High Street stores – who want the best profit margins for their shareholders. And, let's face it, our own greed. We want the cheapest and best bargain we can find in the shops; and we remain blind to the cost to garment workers and others who produce for us in the wealthy western world. No one should have to work hard all day, seven days a week, and then be forced to live in utter squalor because rich people want to be richer.

Advent reflection

'I'm getting a lap-top [computer] for Christmas', I overheard one of my Form at school say. I know her family can ill afford such an unnecessary fashionable gift. Another said, 'Me and my family are going to Goa for Christmas and New Year'. (Presently the fashionable place to be going.) Is this the correct way to be celebrating the birth of Christ, the incarnate Word of God? Do fashion statements celebrate anything but our own blindness? Will either of these students or their families even go to the Eucharist on Christmas Day?

Scripture text

'He will not judge by appearance or hearsay;
    he will judge the poor fairly and defend the rights of the helpless . . .
He will rule his people with justice and integrity.'
Isaiah 11:3-5

Prayer

Almighty God,
    we live in a world that is full of greed,
    yet you loved the world so much,
    that you gave your Son to it.
There must be much good,
    or hope for good in our world.
May I seek that good, live that good
    and encourage that good,
    wherever I find it.
May I have strength from you
    to achieve this. Amen

DAY FIFTEEN

Prophets of human rights

Awoke to the sound of a man chanting over and over again, 'Allah, Allah, Allah' outside, somewhere, in the streets, to the rhythm of the rickshaw bells! It's an Islamic religious festival today, called Shab-e-Barat. At breakfast we met our first Europeans – who aren't really European – two Australians who have never been to Europe! Anyway they seemed like us! Colleen and Bruce are working on a documentary film for use in Australian schools; comparing the life of a 15-year-old Australian girl with her opposite number here. It's the weekend here at the Caritas offices, so much quieter than normal and the streets aren't quite so noisy and thronged.

From 9.30 until 11.30am we met with Father Timm and Rosalind Costa. Father Timm was the director of Caritas and is famous in Dhaka for the many projects that he has been involved with. An American Holy Cross priest, he has been in the country for about 45 years.

Rosalind, a former nun, is deeply committed, courageous (she has to have a bodyguard when she leaves the local area) and a hard-working human rights co-ordinator. Fearlessly she has espoused the cause of the tribal peoples and also the garment workers. Her stories were gripping and disturbing. The official Catholic Church finds her, and her advocacy work, an embarrassment because she is outspoken and exposes injustice whilst tirelessly pursuing hundreds of legal cases against unjust employers, factory owners and landowners. She has been beaten up a number of times and nowadays has to have a bodyguard!

Rosalind and Father Timm have set up 'Hotline Bangladesh', a monthly newsletter which is posted to people or sent by e-mail; it exposes human rights infringements and injustices and copies go to Amnesty International and similar organisations. The latest issue, of which we received a copy, has the heading 'Open Horrible Murders on the Rise'.

We spent the remainder of the morning and the afternoon writing our reports. We had all been invited to tea at Anna and John's home (Anna Minj is Director of the Independent Women's Development Project; her husband is a lawyer). It was our first visit to a middle-class home. In Britain we would class it as a small flat of three rooms, not well decorated and simply furnished. We met Anna and John's two children, a boy and a girl, and their hospitality was overwhelming; loads of tasty nibbles and morsels were forced upon us. It was clear that each of the rooms doubled as a bedroom.

From there we were escorted to Subash's home (another of Caritas' dedicated workers who, like several other young men we had met, had spent some years in the seminary training for the priesthood). We met his lovely, very pregnant wife, and her sister who lives with them. Their little three-room flat was simpler, poorly decorated and, from a west-European point of view poorly furnished; but they showed it off to us with pride and we made appreciative comments. Here too hospitality in the way of food and drink was forced upon us.

After dinner we continued working on our composite report until 10.40pm, a difficult task after the food we had consumed at our two visits.

Reflection

The issue raised today was whether the Church should be prophetic and speak out courageously against injustices and the abuse of basic human rights; or whether it should, as the leadership of the Bangladesh Church appears to do, according to Father Timm and Rosalind Costa, play safe and remain quiet for fear of damaging Church-State relations in an Islamic country. A perennial problem that has haunted the Church since the time of Constantine.

I'm inclined to believe that the Church should stand courageously against injustice wherever it is found, trusting in Christ's promise that he would always be with his community. However, I can understand why the archbishop and the hierarchy take the stance that they do.

Advent reflection

The prophets of old spoke of the coming Messiah; in Isaiah 9:6 it says that he would be called 'wonderful counsellor'; as indeed Christ was. Other prophetic figures since have been and are wonderful advisors and counsellors. At our baptism we were all anointed to be 'priest, prophet and king'. How rarely we pray for the gift of wisdom that we might be wise counsellors and prophetic in speaking out against injustice. How faithfully *am* I living my call to be a prophet?

Scripture text

For to us a child is born . . .
And he will be called Wonderful Counsellor, Mighty God,
    Everlasting Father, Prince of Peace.
    Of the increase of his government and peace there will be no end.
Isaiah 9:6-7

Prayer

Almighty Father,
I feel so low and dispirited;
Nothing I do seems to succeed
    or come out right.
People aren't interested in me
    or what I do.
I need help and advice;
I need to feel the warmth of your love,
    which I know is there.
I need the wisdom to recognise
    where my true strengths and weaknesses lie.
To know who are true friends and good advisors.
Be to me, Lord, a wonderful counsellor,
    a mighty God and everlasting Father. Amen

DAY SIXTEEN

Defending the tribals

Up at 7am after another disturbed night and fitful sleep, which I'm getting accustomed to. We've packed our bags and we're off at 8.30 to Mymensingh in the north. Cathy, Stephen and I are going by road, the others are flying to Rajshahi. We've been in Bangladesh for two weeks and I notice that I've become accustomed to the bells and horns in the street outside my window. Evidently there were religious celebrations going on throughout the night but they didn't disturb me too much – just the occasional fire-cracker!

On the journey north the roads were much quieter, although much business was still being conducted at the roadside markets. The country-side is different in the north; fewer ponds, waterways and rivers; and many big fields of rice. We saw black buffalos, with great big horns, pulling carts or ploughing; and the harvesting of the rice was also in progress. Once or twice we remarked to one another, particularly when going through a wooded area, that this was similar to England. The journey took two-and-a-half hours and we were welcomed at the Caritas Mymensingh offices by Chitta, the regional director, and his staff.

After lunch we set off for an hour's drive to the south-west; we turned off the road onto a forest track and into the Modhupur forest. The driver spoke to the forestry guard who opened a low gate to allow us to enter. It is one of the last forests of Bangladesh. (In 1927, 20 per cent of the country was covered by forest; now only 6 per cent is left.) We were on our way to visit a mission of the indigenous tribal people called the Garos – although they call themselves the Mandi, which means 'human beings'. Their very existence is constantly threatened by the majority Bengali population who are cutting down and despoiling the forest. (The Mandi people, who were formerly animists, are now 98 per cent Christian, mainly Catholic.) We bumped from side to side, as our 4 x 4 jeep made its cautious way along the rutted track. It took 40 minutes, with the forest close on both sides, to reach the village of Pirgacha, where we were surprised to find how settled it all was.

There was a secondary school on our right, a well-appointed priest's house and office equipped with a computer, TV and modern fridge. (Apparently electricity is off their own generator.) The priest who welcomed us is the famous Father Eugene Homrich, who is about 70, but exudes the energy and enthusiasm of a much younger man. An American Holy Cross

Father, he has lived among the Mandi people for 45 years and is an acknowledged expert on the tribals and the Modhupur forest. He took us from his office to his refectory, which was well decorated and full of character (like himself), with tribal drums, weapons, woodcarvings, etc., on the walls. We had tea and cake and Father Homrich said it was a pity that we were only stopping an hour; if we could have stayed a couple of days we could have witnessed the annual native dances to celebrate the harvest. Father Homrich was blunt and outspoken about the corruption in government and the inertia of the Church; he was even critical of Caritas. Several times in the course of the conversation he praised the people of Boston, England, who were twinned with them and provided much appreciated support.

Father Homrich was truly charismatic and spellbinding – you felt that you could sit and listen to him for ever. He was particularly interesting on his work to protect and defend the oppressed Mandi people. He tried to press books and articles on us; we accepted what proved to be a most interesting paper on the history of the tribal people. According to the guidebook we had there are 15,000 Mandi people living in forest villages; however, Father Homrich spoke of 9,500 of whom 6,500 are Catholics. There are 20 primary schools and a secondary school with 160 girls boarding; these are served by 50 trained women teachers or catechists. Several times Father Homrich repeated that the local Church was lay run. (This is a matriarchal society with everything directed from the female side; for example, the daughters inherit the property, children take their mother's name and lineage and at marriage the husbands move into the wives' homes. Men and women enjoy equal positions and equal rights under Mandi social laws.)

Father Homrich said his target was integral human development. He was proud to tell us that literacy among the Mandis is 82 per cent, whereas the national average is 62 per cent. Speaking about himself, Father Homrich said his nickname was 'Father Toilet' because he had campaigned for so long to get proper sanitation everywhere among the tribals. He had sustained 12 motor-cycle accidents over the 45 years and indicated that this side of his body (left shoulder area) was all metal! He was proud of the health care available and boasted of personally delivering about 1,000 babies! He didn't believe in orphanages and had, over the years, placed about 700 orphans with families.

Despite the difficulties there were signs of hope, Father Homrich said; infant mortality rate was down to nearly nil; general health of the population was better and he particularly mentioned the 160 girls in the boarding school (some of whom we met afterwards). He really believed, he said, that the tribals are the Christian hope of the future, because they are so honest and moral; 'What a gift they are to the Church,' he said. In a small and simple shop where Cathy and I both purchased a Garo-designed and woven cloth, Father Homrich pointed out the distinctive Garo design. It is of the eye of God. 'They believe,' he said, 'that God's eye is upon them all the time.'

The visit was over all too soon; an incredible and very memorable experience. We waved goodbye and bumped our way out onto the main road, and back to the Caritas offices.

At dinner, tasty and different from what we had had elsewhere, we met the two Australians again who are filming in this area. Colleen and Bruce, both charming, friendly and very articulate, told us of their experiences filming a 15-year-old married woman and her husband. Caritas had told them that she was 15, which she looked, but the official Government censor, who accompanied them and observed all that they did, insisted that she was 18. Very experienced travellers in Asia, neither Colleen nor Bruce had ever been to Europe. Up in Colleen's room – out of sight of the censor – we shared a bottle of red wine which they had brought with them and for an hour we swapped life stories. Bed a little earlier tonight, at 10.30pm.

Reflection

What a way to follow! The institution of the Church may be falling short of expectations but individual charismatic Christians, like Father Homrich, are certainly making up for it by their clear-sighted enthusiasm. Where would the Mandi people be today but for the dedicated and courageous commitment of one man? It was a wonderful privilege to meet such a priest.

Advent reflection

The Feast of the Incarnation ('the Word was made flesh') which we are preparing to celebrate is, among other things, about the dignity of the individual human person. Almighty God came among us as a new-born human; an incredible belief. Let's repeat it: God took human flesh. By this amazing choice God raised up the dignity of each and every human person. Every human being is priceless. One person, too, can make a difference. By sheer determined commitment and dedication one person can transform and change a situation.

Each of us, for the good of others, can tap into a power that is limitless.

Scripture text

When he comes, he will rule his people with the strength that comes from the Lord and with the majesty of the Lord God himself.
Micah 5:4

Prayer

Father Almighty, I believe.
I believe that you did a truly amazing thing.
I believe that you loved us so much
    that you chose, in the person of your Son,
    to become a poor, weak, human being.
A baby, completely dependent
    upon another weak human being.
When I really stop and think about it
    that is an awesome belief –
    but, with your help, I can and do believe it. Amen

DAY SEVENTEEN

Expectation in the air

It's so much quieter here and I slept well for a change. We were on the road by 8.15am for the long drive to the forest of Jhinaghati and a meeting with two women's groups. The two-hour drive was full of interest: seeing the rice harvest being brought in and where it has, the drying process (often using the roads themselves); and the ploughing, ready for planting the second harvest. (They get three harvests a year from the fields.) It seemed an invasion to drive straight over someone's rice laid out on the roads – but then it shouldn't really be there! At the local Caritas regional office we received the usual warm welcome, but it was a small unit, with only a couple of field officers.

A further short drive brought us to the forest and along very narrow, rough, tracks; eventually they became too narrow and we had to get out and walk the last 400-500 yards to the tiny village which was on the brow of a hill. This was really rural and rustic; we were meeting the Moyur Mohila Samity.* The women's group comprising 16 Garo women in their own colourful traditional dress of skirt and top (not the sari) were sitting waiting for us. (No sign of men anywhere, although various animals, including a tame boar, were sniffing around.) As we have done before, we joined them on the matting and noticed that they each had a pink savings card laid out before them. I asked about these and, with some pride, they told us how they save 10 taka a fortnight; then when enough has been saved they take a loan from the group and set up some small business enterprise, like buying a cow and selling the milk.

We were asked the usual questions about our families and homes; 'Are your houses like ours, made of mud and thatch?' I replied as simply as I could, 'No, they are made of bricks with a slate or tiled roof.' 'That's nice,' the woman responded. They were very sweet people who smiled and laughed a lot. Reluctantly we left their village, in its picturesque setting, and walked down the forest path to our vehicle. (We were very close to the border with India.) The women had told us that at this time of the year, herds of elephants – about 30 at a time – come across from India to raid the rice harvest and have to be driven off. We were a little disappointed not to see any!

The next women's group was just 15 minutes away. Called Protap Nagor Joba Mohila Samity, it comprised a mix of Moslem and Hindu women. The 'vibes' here were different; the group appeared to be poorer,

* Mohila Samity means 'women's group'.

to be unsettled and on edge. As we sat among them and got talking they became more relaxed and opened up. For the first time we had men and loads of children hanging around the fringes of the meeting. (This may have been the reason for the women's lack of ease.) Our guide and interpreter asked the men to move away, but they only took token notice of him. This was not as satisfying an experience as being with the Garo women.

It was a long drive back and there were so many interesting sights for the camera, but lacking the film I just had to try and absorb it all. At 5pm, after the journey, we went to visit the bishop of Mymensigh, Francis Gomes, aged 69. He is Bengali but the Portuguese who converted his ancestors gave their own names to the Bengali people who were received into the Church. He told us about his diocese of a dozen or so parishes with about 3,000 Catholics in each. He is building a new cathedral along-side his house, but work has currently stopped because he has run out of funds. (Bishop Homrich had expressed some caustic comments about the 'concrete monstrosity' being erected, when there were so many other needs!) Father Gomes was friendly and interested in our enterprise, but not so welcoming as the other bishops we had met.

There have been hundreds of sensory experiences today, and a degree of frustration that I could not record all the sights to show family and friends at home: the oxen pulling the ploughs; the rice being harvested by hand; how they lay it out to dry and turn it; the wheelwright at work; the open-sided butcher's stall with meat hanging by the roadside; the school-girls in their smart uniforms of blue-and-white loose trousers and top with a coloured cross-over sash; the jostling rickshaws, etc.

Reflection

The women, in their groups, are certainly impressive and you sense 'expectation' in the air. They are growing in knowledge, understanding and self-assurance. You feel that they are looking to move on; the unasked question is, 'What's next?' Those who spoke of a silent revolution taking place are certainly correct in their judgement.

Advent reflection

The carol says 'How silently, how silently, that wondrous gift is given'. The busy commercial and political world at the moment of Christ's birth had no idea of the amazing event which silently, and almost completely unnoticed, had taken place in a poor stable in a nondescript town in a small Roman province. An event that would revolutionise the world and set higher standards of morality; an event from which all time would be counted.

Scripture text

For a long time I have kept silent,
    I have been quiet and held myself back.
But now, like a woman in childbirth, I cry out, I gasp and pant!
Isaiah 42:14

Prayer

The world is so heavily populated, Lord,
    most of the time I feel so insignificant.
Who am I? What importance do I have?
No wonder people crave to get on TV
    to be seen and admired.
Help me to realise that your coming
    has revealed the dignity of each individual person.
That no one is insignificant and unimportant;
That you love me individually and uniquely,
    and care for me, just *as* I am and *where* I am. Amen

DAY EIGHTEEN

Education, poverty's enemy

Another night of fitful sleep with goods-train noises in the background. It is a beautiful morning – 6.30am – with a wake-up call accompanied by a pail of hot water. Shower and shave in hot water – what a sense of luxury. My first shave in hot water for over two weeks. This morning's weather is just like a sunny English summer's day. (You can't talk about the weather much because every day is virtually the same.)

Here, at Mymensigh, the food is more varied; yesterday we had cooked banana as a vegetable accompanying the inevitable fish (grilled pieces) and, of course, rice. (Banana has also appeared in fried ringlets!) It is 'normal' to encounter frogs leaping along the open terrace outside our rooms but the huge black cockroaches upset Cathy; I just ignore them. There was a largish lizard on the wall above my bed last night; I decided to live and let live and took no notice of it.

We set out for Shadhupara and Judchatra at 8am; so it's back to the Modhupur forest, but a different area. Through the thronged rickshawed streets, jostling with battered buses (with 30 or 40 men sitting on the roofs), and avoiding the colourful heavy lorries who have little inclination to move over for anything smaller than themselves. We again went miles and miles without seeing another car. I tried to get a shot of a butcher's stall with the meat hanging outside, but a lorry trying to avoid a wandering cow in the street got in the way!

We left the reasonably smooth road to bump and bounce along a track for 30 minutes before we arrived at the school. It was heart-stoppingly touching! About 60 very poorly dressed and rather solemn children were lined up in two lines – the youngest (6) in the front. We stood before them as a floral presentation was made to each of us. 'We are poor and can offer you nothing but our flowers, our song and our love.' Then came the song! After this they were marched off to the three simple classrooms in a single-storey, long 'hut' with a corrugated-iron roof which is school. Although the three young teachers were engaged in English lessons with each class, none were prepared to try and speak to us in English; we spoke to the woman headteacher, Ms Shilpi Chanbugong, through the interpreter, although she appeared to understand most of what we were saying. We visited each of the classrooms; the first two had very rough old desks but the youngest children, in the third classroom, sat on matting on the floor. The children were understandably nervous of us as they had not seen white people before. On the blackboard, written in chalk, were the words 'That's a . . .' When I first pointed to a picture in the cheap old textbook (one between three) of a fish, or a pen, there was no response. When I tried saying, 'That's a . . .' the children chorused loudly what it was; so we had a little game and they started giggling and relaxing with us.

This is an Underprivileged Children's Primary Education Programme (UCPEP) school, with earthen floors and walls and no glass in the windows; metal bars cover them. There were no posters or decoration of any kind. We learnt that Caritas pays two of the teachers and the third is paid by the parish. We left our carrier bag full of gifts (colouring pencils, drawing books, etc.) and the headteacher was overwhelmed with pleasure and gratitude. At one point, while waiting for the others to catch up with me, I stepped into a similar building standing at right-angles to the school. The area of earthen floor had a few strips of matting, bare walls, windows with no glass. What, I wondered, is this used for? Then I noticed a very tiny crucifix on the end wall (to the right of the doorway in which I was standing) and in the far corner, on a little shelf, was a statue of the Virgin Mary, about 6 inches high! It suddenly dawned on me, this is the church! I said to the others, surely we could at least get them a decent-size crucifix and statue!

A short walk away (we have done too little walking), we were taken to a weaving centre; the technology could not have been more basic and fundamental. People must have woven cloth like this since the time of Christ. Six of the women from the forest communities were working on spinning wheels – hand-operated, wooden looms stood empty alongside them. We were shown samples of the cloth they weave there; it is an irregular source of income because they have trouble getting materials.

We continued our bumpy journey with the forest almost touching the car on either side; a large monkey scampered across the track in front of us. Arriving at another village where the houses had corrugated-iron roofs, we joined a women's group who were waiting for us. This consisted of 12 self-assured Garo women of the Beduria Mikraka Mohila Samity. We asked the usual questions after introductions, etc., including a question about the corrugated-iron roofs. They said that they were better for keeping out the rain, but noisy and they made the houses hot in the summer and cold in the winter! (I had the clear impression that they regretted parting with thatched roofs.) The women said that they were too shy to ask questions about us; we still told them about our families. In this area, as we travelled we saw lush green countryside where pineapples grew interspersed with banana trees, ginger bushes and jackfruit.

The next community gave us an outstanding welcome, with a prepared programme. First we were met at the entrance to the village by a young girl of about 12 in traditional costume and make-up; behind her were four dancers of about 10 years of age, beautifully attired in red and black. The first girl, slowly walking backwards, strew flower petals on us as the four others danced ahead, with us following. The dance music came from a group sitting in the village 'square' and playing a harmonium and a drum. We were obliged to sit on the chairs that they had provided; the entertainment continued after a short welcoming speech followed by a lovely dance by a girl of about 15 in local Garo costume. This was followed by an unusual dance by a boy a few years younger. He had a 'ball' of white cloth tied round his waist and hanging down behind him – like a big white tail – which, with the movement of his hips, he swung round to and fro to the music as he circled round the group. Next came the bouquets of flowers and our hands were seized, kissed and held to the young woman's forehead! The meeting, as such, then commenced with the customary introductions, explanations and questions. Someone mentioned the local rice wine and two women rushed off to find some for us to try – quite potent! Very sweet tea was served next, in small cups with saucers (nowhere did we see or use mugs; always proper cups and saucers). This very happy, friendly group were not shy with their questions, and with some reluctance we left when our guide told us it was time to move on.

We called at the parish house, formerly Father Homrich's parish, for lunch. The parish priest was out at a meeting but we were entertained by a Sister and a Seminarian. From lunch we went directly to a gathering of the ICDP staff (Integrated Community Development Project) consisting of mainly young people. It was started in 1991 to improve the quality of the lives of the poor and underprivileged Adivasi people who include the tribal groups Garo, Hajong, Koch, Banai, Khotrio, Dalu and Barmans.

These indigenous people are under great pressure – especially finding their ancestral lands being taken by the Government Forestry Department. They have seen their traditional culture eroded. Most of the people that we have met live below the poverty line. There are 484 villages and 1,202 groups who meet to save and learn together. It was quite a large group of young field workers and there was a good sharing of ideas; they asked about our families. It was just a short walk to our next visit, to the silk factory next door. We saw and photographed the bright orange-coloured cocoons and a table covered in silk worms that were eating mulberry leaves. Then we went to the office of Ms Rajshaki, the production manager, who explained how the factory worked. On the tour we saw how basic the technology was, but how skilful the workers were as they spun the thread, dyed it and wove scarves and saris. We admired the ingenious way in which bicycle parts, for example wheels, chains and pedals, were being used to drive the spinning-wheels. A beautiful ruby red wedding sari, with a gold-thread pattern, was being woven; some saris were being block printed while others were being tie-dyed.

Women do the weaving and a skilled weaver can earn up to 3,000 taka a month (equivalent to £10 a week) but the starting pay is 600 taka. Working conditions are a lot better than those of the garment workers; working hours are from 8.30am to 4.30pm, with an hour for lunch and Fridays off. We were shown the crèche/childcare place where I took a few photos of the children. It was actually nothing more than a covered veranda where two young girls watched over eight children ranging from one year to 8 years of age. There were no toys or facilities. The production manager told us that while there were 300 poor women working in the factory there were 8,000 outworkers who contributed by growing the mulberry bushes and extracting the silk from the orange-coloured cocoons when they were ready.

On our return this afternoon we shared a cup of tea with the Australians and both then and at dinner heard about their last day of shooting their educational film. We said goodbye because they leave tomorrow and we will be out and about before them. Lots of flying insects around this evening and although we spent some time on report writing, it was earlier to bed, as we are up at 6am to be on the road an hour later. I'm tucking my mosquito net in more securely tonight as I don't like the look of the hundreds of insects gathering on the bedroom wall!

Reflection

So much to reflect upon today! Perhaps it will be the school for the underprivileged children that I will, above all, remember. Education is understood, here, to be essential; a way out of poverty. Time and again, wherever we've been, we've found a seriousness about education among the children and young people that you don't find in Britain; we all remarked on it. If only the pupils I teach had half the commitment and dedication that these Bangladeshi children have; how their lives would be changed.

Advent reflection

Education develops an individual's potential, self-confidence and sense of personal dignity and worth. Education is incarnational; it raises people up. Advent, like Lent, exists for an educational purpose: to raise our awareness and appreciation of the depth of meaning of the feast of the Incarnation. As St Athanasius said, 'He became what we are that he might make us what he is.'

Scripture text

The Spirit of the Lord will rest on him –
    the Spirit of wisdom and of understanding,
    the Spirit of counsel and of power,
    the Spirit of knowledge and of the fear of the Lord.
Isaiah 11:2

Prayer

Eternal Wisdom,
    you gave us your Word,
    that you might reveal yourself
    more deeply and more endearingly to us.

May I grow in knowledge of your Son,
    and what he revealed of you,
    and of your wonderful love.
May I have the wisdom
    to live by what I learn. Amen

DAY NINETEEN

'Jusuna rasong'

Up just before 6am and greeted with a bucket of hot water at the door; another luxurious wash and shave.

We are going out early so that we can finish at lunchtime and have a little leisure time to write reports before we pack for our return to Dhaka. Our journey today took nearly two hours and although the roads were busy we didn't see a single car for the whole journey to Nabitabari, and back. The women's group (mohila samity) was not ready for us when we arrived so we called on Father Louis Samar of the local parish of Baromari. He is in charge of a Pilgrimage Centre founded there three years ago. After coffee with him on his veranda, and an explanation about the centre, he took us on the Way of the Cross and to the Shrine.

For the first time we were in the hills, close to the northern border with India, which is one kilometre away. (We had passed a border guard camp on the road.) The Way of the Cross consists of tall concrete crosses, covered with white tiles and standing about 10 feet high; they are spaced out over a small hill, with magnificent views all around.

At the top of the hill, Calvary, three equal-size white crosses stand together. The steps up to the top were cut out of the soil; quite hard now, but will probably be washed away in the wet season. Father Louis, who arrived at the shrine in July, is full of enthusiasm and explained that they would probably find a benefactor to pay for concrete steps. I suggested an alternative idea: that every pilgrim is invited to bring a brick with them (bricks are cheap and easily obtained in Bangladesh) and volunteers could lay them. Father Louis thought that was a good idea. He had already told us that the shrine was the brainchild of the Bishop of Mymensigh and in the first year 5,000 Christians had come. This year, the third, there had been 20,000 pilgrims.You could see the appeal of the place – especially if you lived in polluted Dhaka.

We came down off the Way of the Cross into a large cleared flat area, a type of arena, where the shrine is. The large statue of Our Lady of Fatima, and the altar in front of it, is surprisingly high up in a large pagoda-type structure at the top of about 12 to 14 steps. We climbed up and peered through the steel security gates that surround it when not in use. At the foot of the steps, to the right, a simple spring pours water through a pipe into a hole in the ground. Father Louis told us that the spring had started since they had completed the shrine and pilgrims liked to take some of the water home. (Echoes of Lourdes?) The priest made light of it, but told us that pilgrims have already claimed two cures from the water.

We walked in the sunshine, enjoyed the beautiful scenery and appreciated the exercise, which we have had little of on this trip. We could hear the parish school before we came round the hillside and down to where it was; primary and secondary together. We missed the senior students, who were just pouring out for break, so we visited and talked to the junior children in two classrooms. They found us interesting! Ascending the hill again we returned to the priest's house, where one of the religious sisters who run the school told us that a welcoming presentation by some of the Garo children in their tribal costume, was ready for us. Ten girls in red costumes with silver head-dresses, a feather in each head-dress, danced to the music of a harmonium played by the sister, and a drum played by a male teacher. After the lovely song and two dances the girls presented us with posies of flowers. We all posed for a photo together and when I told the older ones who were about 12 years of age that I would show their picture to my 15-year-old son, they ran off in convulsions of giggling! Here, at the Pilgrimage Centre, we were introduced to the Christian greeting 'Jusuna rasong' which means, 'In the name of Jesus'.

On to the Kharuma Mohila Samity and another great welcome! 'We have nothing to give you,' they said, '*but* our song and our flowers.' It was very humbling again. After the song and the flowers we sat down with them in their circle and then followed one of the best discussions that we have had anywhere. This was a mature group who were relaxed with us. There was as much laughter as serious questions and answers. All 22 women sitting there were married, apart from two. Two of the mothers carried on breast-feeding their children (one of whom must have been 18 months or more, because he walked off afterwards!). They just pushed the child's head up under their tops and kept on talking. We took no notice as we had seen it in other groups, and what with the occasional chicken strolling through the centre of the circle and a tame boar snorting around on the grass alongside us, this was now commonplace.

One of the single women, Carmella Jenchan (22), told us about the second-hand Singer sewing machine that she had bought with a loan from the group. She insisted on taking us into her mud-constructed home, to show us. She had saved 250 taka (10 taka a fortnight) and then was able to borrow the 2,500 needed to buy the machine. She was so proud of it. In her little earthen-floor home we asked her to show us how she used it. She pulled the stand away from the wall and beneath a large picture of the Sacred Heart of Jesus (this was mainly a Christian group), she demonstrated how she made little tops and underskirts. 'I've got 24 orders,' she told us proudly. Apparently local women get the material themselves and come along to her and tell her what they want made. Like everyone else we had met, these women were landless and worked for the local landowner. For bringing in the rice harvest, they told us they would be paid 30 taka a day – their menfolk got 40 taka. We asked if this wasn't unfair. One replied, 'Not really, because the men have the additional job of carrying heavy loads up to the roads.'

Outside Carmella's family home I was introduced and spoke to her father who, with her brother, was making a wooden door. They were doing their carpentry squatting down – as everyone does in this country. I told him that my grandfather was a woodworker and used similar tools to those he had beside him. Before we left we met Rakhi Mrong, a young field-worker for Caritas; she arrived on a Honda motorcycle with her traditional clothes tucked up out of the way. She told us that she had 130 groups like this one to take care of; she tried to visit two a day. This was our last group visit; and one of the best.

The long journey back provided us with all the usual interesting sights. I wanted to get a photo of one of the painted lorries and just missed an opportunity at a place visible from the road where they were being painted by a couple of artists. I didn't like to ask our driver to stop. After a restful hour back at the Caritas regional headquarters, we settled down to writing our reports – Cathy and I eventually finished at 10pm.

Reflection

The peace of the pilgrimage centre and the pride of Carmella will be my abiding memory of today; rich as it was in experiences. Carmella, as a Catholic probably named after Our Lady of Mount Carmel, showed such pride in her achievements. Father Louis was proud of the centre for Our Lady of Fatima. It is good to witness genuine sincere pride.

Advent reflection

Mary, the simple peasant girl from Nazareth, now known as 'Our Lady of Mount Carmel', 'Our Lady of Fatima', etc., must have faced the prospect of delivering a baby on her own – with Joseph's help – with fear and trembling. Having a baby, even in perfectly controlled hospital conditions, is frightening enough; but in a stable! What pride she must have had in her achievement on that first Christmas morning. Let's not be so focused on the baby that we forget Mary.

Scripture text

And Mary said:
'My soul glorifies the Lord and my spirit rejoices in God my Saviour,
for he has been mindful of the humble state of his servant.
From now all generations will call me blessed.'
Luke 1:46, 47

Prayer

Father of Mary and Joseph,
and our Father too,
as we recall the events
leading up to the birth of your Son,
may we not forget
the wonderful obedience to your will,
of Mary of Nazareth.
Without her there would have been no Christmas!
Without her humility
we would all still be
in the darkness of human pride and sin.
May her example inspire
and guide us in our own efforts
to find and do your will. Amen

DAY TWENTY

'Thank you' time

A much better night's sleep, and – thank God – the joy of a bucket of hot water at the door, at 6.45am. I've started to pack for our departure today for the polluted city.

So, after nearly three hours of travel we are back in Dhaka; the chaos on the roads and the traffic jams are almost unbelievable. No one is prepared to give way to anyone else! It's much hotter here and the polluted air is noticeable. No wonder the policemen on traffic control (there's an oxymoron!) wear facemasks. We saw lots of grimy looking garment sweatshops, above the actual small 'shops' and businesses fronting the pavement. People, like schoolchildren in their uniforms, walk in the roads because the pavements, if you can call them that, are clogged and unusable.

Before we left Mymensingh, Cathy and I went with an interpreter to call on the Catholic school next door to Caritas. We were looking for a photograph of the girls in their school uniforms, to show pupils back home. We also interviewed one of the high school students, Runa Mrong (16). She told us about her family of five sisters and two brothers; and the subjects that she studies. When Cathy asked her what she would like to do after college and a degree, she surprised us when she said, quite directly, 'I would like to be a nun.'

We had a short chat with the Sister Superior, who explained that they were not Salesian Sisters, founded by St John Bosco, but De Sales Sisters founded by St Francis De Sales. She told us that their real name incorporates the word 'Missionaries', but they had to drop that part of their title because the Muslims thought they were there to try to convert them. We returned to the Caritas compound and shortly afterwards met with the whole regional staff of about 40 people.

Each of us on the CAFOD team spoke of our impressions of Bangladesh and the development projects we had visited. We praised the wonderful welcome and warm hospitality that we had received everywhere and the high standard of professionalism that we had encountered from each and every member of the Caritas staff. We were each presented with a gift; mine was a length of beautiful green and red cloth woven by the Garo women. After a final coffee with the regional director (who we later learnt had been a freedom fighter in the 1971 war against Pakistan) we said our goodbyes.

We got back to Dhaka about midday, long before the others, and took the opportunity to visit the Catholic National Youth Office who have premises on the Caritas site. The National chaplain was keen to tell us about the youth groups they run and the problems that they encounter. I asked about inner-city work with the young garment workers, but it emerged that most of their activities are with students. In the course of conversation about sexual behaviour and preparation for marriage, we learnt that about 50 per cent of marriages – even among Christians – are still arranged. Statistics have revealed that the arranged marriages are more enduring!

We started to get anxious when our colleagues had not returned on time and rumours of all sorts of delays started circulating; however, at about 6pm they turned up safely and in good spirits. We then had to get ourselves ready for the 'last supper'! Stephen, our leader, had arranged a final 'thank you' meal for all the Caritas staff and other NGOs who had made our visit so wonderfully productive. Chris and Steve had been given, as parting gifts from their last visit, traditionally decorated long white shirts and they looked splendid in them. Anne-Marie wore a sari, and looked great. Cathy and I were just neat and tidy in the best items that we had that were still clean! I put socks and shoes on for the first time in three weeks. In a minibus we set out for the Panda Garden Chinese restaurant; it should have taken 15 minutes to cross the city but it actually took an hour in absolutely horrendous traffic. (No one at home would believe the chaos we have witnessed on the roads.) The gentleman from NGO Forum, with his daughter, sat next to me during the meal and pleaded with me to return to Bangladesh and bring my family. I said that it would be quite expensive to do that and he replied that he had two rooms in his home that we could use!

Opposite me sat the director of Corr, the jute works, that we had visited at the beginning of the visit. Almost opposite me was Sister Eugenia who wanted me to write to a Centre in Cambridge about an award that she had been promised. It was a very pleasant meal and over all too soon. There were short speeches from Stephen King, our leader, and Mr Bitu D'Costa, the Director of Caritas, with mutual praises and thanks. On the journey back, which took 20 minutes, Rosalind Costa told us that the 'baby taxi' drivers hire the vehicle for 200 taka for half a day and hope to take 500 taka, making a profit of 300 taka which is considerably more than a rickshaw puller makes.

Reflection

We have been recipients of kindness and generosity every day. Not a day has gone by without a constant need to say 'thank you'. True, all the agencies, directors and workers have been out to impress us, in the hope of continuing support from CAFOD for their projects. But, taking that into account, the warmth of the welcome everywhere has been sincere and the sharing of ideas genuine. The meal was the least we could do to express our thanks.

Advent reflection

Advent and Christmas should prompt us to say 'thank you'. It is traditionally a time when people give bottles of wine, boxes of chocolates, etc., to express gratitude for some service rendered during the previous year. How much more is it the opportunity to say a big 'thank you' to our God, who freely, in his immeasurable generosity and love, gave us the most precious service of all: the gift of his Son to be with us and available to us all the time; not just through one year.

Scripture text

Since we are receiving a kingdom that cannot be shaken, let us be thankful, and so worship God acceptably with reverence and awe.
Hebrews 12:28

Prayer

On the whole, Lord,
   we are not particularly good
   at saying 'thank you'.
Yes, we are prompt to ask for help,
   and turn to you in need.
But the 'thank you' prayer
   is often left unsaid.
May we use the opportunity
   of this Christmas
   to say a heartfelt 'thank you'
   for your daily help throughout the last year.
And may I be better at expressing
   my gratitude in the coming year. Amen

DAY TWENTY-ONE

Dedicated commitment

Suddenly the last day is here and with it the desire to go home. I've been waking every morning at 4am for some odd reason and then dozed fitfully until getting-up time. This morning we were allowed a lie-in until 7.30am! Back here in Dhaka my voice and throat are being affected again – I shan't miss this polluted city. Our group had its own meeting for an hour after breakfast, to sort out what we were each going to say and what questions we might ask when we met with the directors of Caritas later in the morning. We also had to sort out the monies covering the artefacts we bought *and* get our passports back. There is still some confusion about the actual time of the flight home.

We met for two hours with the Caritas executives. We each made a little speech praising the planning and organisation during our three-week visit and the hospitality we had enjoyed everywhere. After lunch and some time to ourselves, we went out for a trip on the river. To reach the riverside we had to go through the old town which was busy and congested but, we were told, not as busy as it usually is, as it is Friday. There were market traders, especially for clothes, along the kerbsides; piles of dates and sweetmeats were for sale, often covered in flies. The old town has some buildings that were once substantial and imposing but now are very run down; beggars were tap, tap, tapping on the car window and poverty stared you in the face, wherever you looked.

We alighted at the waterfront and pushed our way through a curious throng to where numerous open wooden boats, each with an oarsman at the helm, were plying their trade. When they saw we were looking for transport they started shouting out to us. Big rusting passenger ferries, six or eight of them, were moored up. There was lots of activity all around and people stopping in their tracks to stare at us. In the jostling crowds I kept one hand on my camera and one in the pocket where my wallet was. With the aid of a man in uniform – no idea who or what he was – we hired and clambered down into two boats. Five went in one and three of us went in the other. It was a rocking, wooden, shallow-draught boat. The oarsman, I learnt through the interpreter, owned the boat, which is normally used to ferry people across the river (there's no bridge). On this occasion he gave us a half-hour trip up the river to see the sights – and so many of them! There was almost the same chaos on the river, with similar boats coming at you from all angles, as on the roads; how the many boats don't crash into one another I have no idea. After our 'cruise' and photos of the sights, we landed with some serious risk of falling in the evil-looking mud at the water's edge.

Back in our eight-seater people carrier we headed for Arong, a 'posh', up-market shop to do our last bit of shopping. This was the one and only European-style shop that we had visited in three weeks. Rather like a small department store, it had a wide range of goods on different floors. I was looking for a gift for my son, Tom, as I already had gifts for the women-folk. I found a model rickshaw made of brass, which seemed quite suitable and paid 820 taka for it (about £11). Outside the shop we decided that this was our last chance to have a photo of a rickshaw. Just up the road we found several rickshaws waiting for customers. Our interpreter asked one if he would allow us to take a photograph of us sitting in his rickshaw; the photos were taken and then Steve and I interviewed him.

His name is Delwar Hussein and he is 35; he has a wife and two daughters. They came into the city a year ago because they could not make enough money to survive living in the countryside. He told us that he hired the rickshaw for eight hours each day, either from 5am or from 2pm, for 44 taka. He hopes to earn 80 taka or more from his work. We gave him a tip for his trouble, but I felt absolutely dreadful because I had just come out of a shop where I had spent 820 taka on a gift! This incident alone points up how vast the gap is between the rich and the poor. I'll never forget this experience.

After a cup of tea, back at Caritas, we reviewed the day and went to pack. It's now after supper and a final briefing in a few minutes; we must be up early for a 3.30am departure. My bag is packed and I'm constantly thinking now of home. My watch has stopped – it needs a new battery – so I'm reliant on a call from our leader. I'm hoping to get a few hours of sleep before we depart.

Reflection

It was a humbling day. The dedicated professionalism of the highly quali-fied Caritas directors still comes across very powerfully. I had never dreamt, back home, that such well-educated and dedicated people were working so purposefully for the poor in this developing country. My other abiding memory from today will be the humbling meeting with the rickshaw puller.

Advent reflection

After 'love' the virtue most in evidence at Christmas is 'humility'. We cannot wonder enough at our belief that the Creator of the vast Universe chose to become a human being on tiny planet Earth. And then as a helpless baby! If that is not humility, what is? Yes, we express our love for our family and friends with gifts and time spent with them; but what about humility? How can I be more humble this Christmas?

Scripture text

He has performed mighty deeds with his arm;
    he has scattered those who are proud in their inmost thoughts.
He has brought down rulers from their thrones
    but has lifted up the humble.
Luke 1:51, 52

Prayer

Loving Father,
    you could hardly have chosen
    a more humble couple
    than Mary and Joseph
    to effect your own plan of humility.
In my proud, arrogant and assertive moments
    may I recall this incredible humility
    of my Creator, my Saviour –
    and Mary and Joseph. Amen

DAY TWENTY-TWO

Going home

We're going home! It was a long 'night' because although I dozed off a couple of times I didn't seem to sleep much, and I had no idea what the time was.

After a call and a very quick cold shower I was the first downstairs at 3.15am for a cup of tea before we left. We loaded two cars, one with the luggage and one with ourselves; we were accompanied by four of the Caritas staff, to see us off. The streets were not completely deserted – some tea stalls were open and a few rickshaws appeared to be about. Goods were coming into the wholesale vegetable market on lorries. When we got to the airport terminal there was a surprising number of men milling around, for what purpose was not clear. We entered an almost deserted terminal and were soon through to the departure lounge. We stopped after 30 minutes at Calcutta and sat in the plane for an hour before our journey continued. The flight on BA144 was quite comfortable but seemed much longer than the flight out.

We eventually landed at Heathrow at 1.30pm and said quite quick goodbyes, as Cathy was met by friends and Chris by his fiancee. Steve and Anne-Marie went off to find their flight to Manchester and Stephen King and I shared a taxi to Liverpool Street station. We'll meet up again next in a few weeks at Preston to put the finishing touches to our report for the Millennium Commission.

Looking out on London from the taxi, everything seemed quite weird after three weeks in a different culture. I tried to sleep on the train to Southend but I was too hyped up and couldn't wait to see Liz and the family again. Met at 5.15pm by Liz at Victoria station, Southend; so pleased to be home, but so grateful too for the incredible experience I'd been fortunate to have.

Reflection

There's no place like home. Although I thought several times, while in Bangladesh, how good it would be to live there and have a much simpler life-style, serving people in need, I know that I wouldn't be able to take my family; and, anyway, I would never really cope with the reality of life there, especially in the hot and steamy season.

Advent reflection

It's a long walk from Nazareth to Bethlehem, and Mary, very uncomfortable in the last stages of her pregnancy must have been so relieved to see the lights of the town in the early evening. How shattered she must then have been to find that there was no accommodation available for her and her husband. Hardly an auspicious start to a night of labour. The joy and the triumph, and the visit of the shepherds came later. Is it not often the case that pain and suffering have to come first? Twelve years later, Mary and Joseph endured three nights of pure agony, looking for the lost Jesus; until there was joy and triumph, when they found him in the Temple. Some 20 years after that, the same Jesus had to endure the agony and the suffering of the cross, before the glory and the triumph of the resurrection. That same Risen Christ is with us this Christmas; the message has not changed.

Scripture text

Simeon said to Mary, 'This child is destined to cause the falling and rising of many in Israel, and to be a sign that will be spoken against, so that the thoughts of many hearts will be revealed. And a sword will pierce your own soul too.'
Luke 2:34, 35

Prayer

Lord, we are wishing one another
    a 'happy Christmas'
    but for so many people
    it will not be a happy time.
And, even in our own homes,
    it is not a time of constant joy and jollity.
Mary and Joseph found that
    it was a happy experience for only part of the day.
But human life is like that:
    we often have to courageously endure,
    before we can celebrate.
May the spirit of the Risen Christ
    be always with us to give us
    the courage in adversity
    and the hope and expectation of glory. Amen

DAY TWENTY-THREE

Afterthoughts and aftershock

Although I don't really feel like it, I've decided to keep the diary going for another day or two, just to record my adjustment to culture shock. I'm not due back into school until Wednesday, so I've got a couple of days to rest and unwind. Although I felt shattered last evening, because I hadn't slept really well for quite a long time, and from leaving Caritas in Dhaka to arriving home (I couldn't sleep on the plane) was about 20 hours of travel, I was too hyped up to rest. I insisted on getting out all my presents, artefacts, etc., to share with the family who had all gathered to welcome me home. There was a sari each for Liz and the three girls and the model of a rickshaw for Tom. Everyone was interested and keen to hear about whatever came into my head to tell them! It was incredibly wonderful to lie back and soak in a hot bath and have a really English dinner of chicken casserole.

I didn't feel ready this morning (Sunday) to face the questions and interest of the parishioners of my local church so I went to a neighbouring parish, only to be spotted by three of my Form. I slipped out of the church during the last hymn to avoid them! There'll be time enough to tell my Form all about it when I return to school. The 'flatness' that I feel today is almost certainly due to still being tired . . . I woke at 4am again for some inexplicable reason. My body clock will no doubt take a while to sort itself out.

Reflection

'Home is where your heart is', so the saying goes. There's no doubt that I'm glad to be back to the security of my family and home; but I've left a little bit of my heart back in Bangladesh. I keep thinking, quite emotionally on occasion, of the people I met; people who were so kind and loving to us.

Advent reflection

Where was Mary's heart as she approached Bethlehem? Was it back in Nazareth with her parents and family, or just where she uncomfortably was, with Joseph in a strange town? Probably a bit of both. As a young expectant mother, in unfamiliar and almost hostile surroundings, Mary must have craved security. And Joseph must have been yearning to provide it for her. Once the baby was born the Holy Family would be going through a time of continual insecurity; even just avoiding a murderous and jealous king. Whatever insecurity and danger we experience, it is worth remembering that God, in Christ Jesus, has been there first.

Scripture text

So Joseph also went up from the town of Nazareth in Galilee to Judea, to Bethlehem the town of David . . . While they were there, the time came for the baby to be born, and she gave birth to her firstborn, a son.
Luke 2:4-6

Prayer

Heavenly Father, in the crib we see
    a peaceful, attractive tableau
    that hides the real truth.
The stable would not have been comfortable,
    the noise and the smell of the animals
    would not have been pleasant
    as the young mother tried to sleep
    after the exhaustion of giving birth.
But you were there,
    giving patience, perseverance and courage.
Bringing happy visitors to cheer
    and encourage.
The young couple not only survived
    the ordeal, but gave the world a saviour.
May we take the lesson to heart;
    you are always with us,
    always ready to give us patience,
    perseverance and courage – if we but ask. Amen

DAY TWENTY-FOUR

Contrasts

I took my nine films in to Mr Collin, our local chemist, this morning; I'm really looking forward to getting the photos back. It's pretty essential, otherwise I won't be able to remember what happened where and in what sequence; I'm already beginning to mix events up. I'm so glad that I made the effort every evening to write my personal diary, the three weeks went so quickly and it was such a precious experience. I've done little else but sit around today; just don't seem to have any energy. I've worked through a pile of post, without any enthusiasm or much interest; our lives here seem to be so cluttered up with things. I step into the garage – a mini-warehouse – where no car has ever resided, and ask myself, 'Do we really need all this stuff?' A family of five, where I've been, live in an area the size of my garage! I must not fall into the temptation of continually contrasting things; our culture and society is the way it is, I can't change it, and it has developed into this over a long period of time. Their culture is the way it is, and sadly I can do nothing about that either. I can only help people here to be more aware.

While in Bangladesh I wrote the following notes in the back of my diary:

Contrasts
- the polluted air of Dhaka . . . and the freshness of the fields and country-side
- the constant noise of the cities . . . and the peace and tranquillity of the Pilgrimage centre
- the hoardings advertising computer courses . . . above street-mothers and children washing their clothes in gutter water
- the few, very few, high-powered Toyotas . . . the many, very many leg-aching rickshaw pullers
- the garish city cinema adverts . . . the simple melody and dance of the Mandi people
- the tearing hurry of the overcrowded buses . . . the plodding ox carts
- the brutality of the acid-throwing that we have heard of . . . the wonderful gentleness and kindness we experienced everywhere
- the highly decorated and individually painted heavy lorries . . . the plain, wooden, handcarts laboriously drawn or pushed by gaunt men
- the dignity of the placid silk weavers . . . the harassed eyes of the young garment workers

– the many young fieldworkers with masters' degrees . . . the illiterate poor of village and slum
– the environmental awareness of the forest dwellers . . . the rapacious double-dealings of the Forestry Commission.

Reflection

Meeting Christ in Bangladesh
I met Christ
– in the gentle smiles and welcome of all: Hindu, Muslim and Christian
– in the patient struggles of the poor
– in the tenacity of the womenfolk
– in the almost tangible hope of the village groups
– in the evident thirst for knowledge and education
– in the dedication of the field officers of Caritas and the other agencies
– in the inspiring example of spiritual leaders, like Father Homrich
– in the other Holy Cross priests, and the Bangladesh bishops and priests
– in the Eye-of-God symbol of the Garo people, with their 'super conscience'.

Bangladesh is an Advent country, a country of hope struggling to come to birth.

Advent reflection

There was an empty stable; then a stable with a poor tired couple. Then a stable with a young woman, alone with her husband, struggling to give birth to her first baby. Then there was a happy family scene, with a proud but exhausted couple and a sleeping baby. There was peace.

Now there is the goodness of the poor but cheerful shepherds; but the evil of the world crashes in as a murderous king sends his troops to hunt the child. Now the innocent, frightened family seek safety as refugees in a foreign land. And we are back to normal!

Scripture text

'Get up,' the angel said, 'take the child and his mother and escape to Egypt. Stay there until I tell you . . .'
Matthew 2:14

Prayer

Almighty Father,
 this is a wondrous time of the year,
 but you would not want us
 to over-sentimentalise or romanticise
 the reality of your Son's birth,
 to poor guardians in harsh circumstances.
Bless us and those we love
 this Christmas and help us
 to never cease wondering
 at the real mystery of this season,
 at your incredible love
 that prompted you to give
 your very self to us,
 with such generosity and humility. Amen